DISCARDED

POLICY STUDIES IN EMPLOYMENT AND WELFARE NUMBER 16

General Editors: Sar A. Levitan and Garth L. Mangum

Chicanos and Rural Poverty

Vernon M. Briggs, Jr.

The Johns Hopkins University Press, Baltimore and London

The Johns Hopkins University Press, Baltimore, Maryland 21218
The Johns Hopkins University Press Ltd., London

Library of Congress Catalog Card Number 72–12370
ISBN 0–8018–1473–1 (cloth)
ISBN 0–8018–1472–1 (paper)

Library of Congress Cataloging in Publication data will be found on the last printed
page of this book.

Contents

v

Preface

The majority of Chicanos—as is true of blacks and Anglos —reside and work in the urban American economy. Yet it is a constant source of serious error to conclude from such a statement that the rural population is insignificant in number and that the rural economy is inconsequential in importance. To the contrary, in 1970, a total of 53.8 million people resided in "officially" classified rural areas. The figure is virtually identical with the number for 1960. Similarly, there were 23.3 million people in 1970 who were employed in nonmetropolitan areas (an *increase* of 3.4 million workers over the 1960 level). Thus, despite the attention given to our cities in the last decade, a proper perspective for social welfare studies must encompass both the urban and the rural sectors of the economy.

Likewise, any serious investigation of the dimensions of poverty in the United States must definitely include the rural populace. The Bureau of the Census reports that 49 percent of the persons listed as composing the poverty population in 1969 resided in nonmetropolitan areas.

As will be shown in this volume, the lives and welfare of a disproportionately high number of Chicanos are affected by developments in the rural economy. This group and this relationship are the subjects of the present inquiry. The study does not seek to perpetuate the myth that Chicanos as a group are tied intrinsically to the events of the rural sector; most are not. Nonetheless, many Chicanos are, and will be, in this situation for some time to come.

The Chicanos of America are geographically concentrated in the Southwest. Their high rate of rural poverty has assumed a character that is distinctly different from the poverty of other regions and other groups. Any hope for possible resolution of their plight must begin with the recognition of these differences.

This policy paper is an outgrowth of a project conducted for the Center for the Study of Human Resources at The University of Texas at Austin in conjunction with a U.S. Office of Economic Opportunity grant to study rural poverty in the South. The encouragement provided by F. Ray Marshall, director of the center, is sincerely appreciated. The work of Stephen Gaskins, who served as my graduate assistant during the period when much of the background material was gathered, is also acknowledged. The typing and editorial work of Susie Turner, Linda Beaver, and Charlotte Smith were crucial to the evolution of the final draft. To these people, and to my patient wife Martijna, I am grateful.

V.M.B.

Austin, Texas
September 1972

Chicanos and Rural Poverty

1

General Background

INTRODUCTION

In the pursuit of a more equitable and humane society, events of the 1960s and 1970s have required that public attention in the United States be directed upon the welfare of various subgroups within the overall population. Although aggregate barometers of economic progress soared to unparalleled heights of prosperity, sectoral indicators often revealed differential lags and significant voids that spelled little change for significant numbers of citizens. Much of the unrest within the nation during this period has emanated from these people who have been "left behind" and from their empathizers. The shortcomings of economic averages were expressed by former Secretary of Labor Willard Wirtz: "If you put one hand in a deep freeze and the other in the flame of a stove, you are on the average just right; but your extremities are in no end of pain." Such is the nature of "the paradox of poverty among plenty" as the nation approaches its 200th year.

Compared to the void of the past, unprecedented steps have been initiated in recent years to respond to those who comprise the "extremities" of our society. Manpower programs have been launched, regional development discussed, equal employment legislation adopted, and a "war on poverty" proclaimed. Yet, a postreview of actual happenings reminds one of the old adage that "after all is said and done, more is said than done." The mainstays of national economic policy have continued to be fiscal and monetary policies. While these policies were slightly embroidered by the new programs in the sixties, the fundamental institutional reforms so desperately needed were and still are counted as not important enough for serious consideration. Attention centers upon growth of the economic superstructure while the underpinnings of the economy continue to rot for lack of structural repair.

A prime example of the incongruity between the direction of public economic policy and the needs of human beings is the treatment of the Chicano population of rural America. This group is the subject of this volume.

THE IDENTITY ISSUE

Every study of "white persons of Spanish-speaking surname" (the term used by U.S. Census) begins with a taxonomic debate. Exactly who within this broad statistical category is being discussed? Carey McWilliams, noted authority on the settlement process in the Southwest, has written of the identity problem of Chicanos:

Any phrase selected to characterize the Spanish-speaking will necessarily prove to be misleading, inaccurate, or possibly libelous. If there is a generally accepted usage it is to be found in the phrase "Spanish-speaking," but many people speak Spanish who cannot be identified with the Spanish-speaking group. Besides, the people who are generally Spanish-speaking are more Indian in racial origin, and perhaps in culture, than they are Spanish. "Latin American" is vague and euphemistic; "Spanish American" detracts from the importance of the Mexican and Indian heritage; while "Mexican American" implies a certain condescension.[1]

2

In addition, there are numbers of citizens who are Spanish-speaking from Puerto Rico, Cuba, the Philippines, South America, and Europe. Table 1 indicates the estimated size and origin of the Spanish-American population of the United States in 1969. By far, those of Mexican descent dominate the group. Totaling over 5.1 million people in 1969 (with unofficial estimates totaling as high as 7.5 million in 1971) they deserve more public attention as a group than they presently receive. In fact, those of Mexican origin exceed in number the combined total of all nonblack minority groups (i.e., Puerto Ricans, Cubans, American Indians, Chinese Americans, and Japanese Americans).

For present purposes, this study centers almost exclusively upon those people of Mexican descent who reside in five southwestern states (Texas, New Mexico, Colorado, Arizona, and California). These are the Chicanos. Support for the term "Chicano" as used in this study comes from a 1970 statement by Commissioner Vincente T. Ximenes of the Equal Employment Opportunity Commission and a former president of the American G.I. Forum:

> The word "Chicano" is being used by Mexican Americans of the nation. The word is not new and, in fact, we used it to identify the people of the small rural villages many years ago. It is derived from the word Mexicano. I favor its usage.[2]

(The word itself is a derivative of the word "Mexicano" with the first syllable dropped and the "x" pronounced like "ch" in church; its origin stems from the rural Indians of Mexico who pronounced "Mexicano" as "Meh-chee-cano" and then later shortened the word to "Chicano.")

José Angel Gutierrez, a leader of the Mexican American Youth Organization (MAYO) in Texas, has expressed it this way: " 'Chicano' is just to say that we are neither Mexican nor American, we are in between."[3]

3

Table 1. Origin or descent of the Spanish-American population, November, 1969

Origin or descent	Number of people	Percent
Mexican	5,073,000	55.0
Puerto Rican	1,454,000	15.8
Cuban	565,000	6.1
Central or South American	556,000	6.0
Other Spanish American	1,582,000	17.1
Total	9,230,000	100.0

NOTE: Inmates of institutions and members of the armed services are *excluded*.
SOURCE: "Spanish American Population: November, 1969," *Current Population Reports*, series P-20, no. 195 (February 20, 1970), p. 2.

The Chicano population is both a racial and an ethnic minority. It has been estimated that 95 percent of the Chicano population are part Indian and 40 percent are full-blooded Indian, with those of mixed blood usually more Indian than not.[4] Although the implied accuracy of such racial percentages is open to question, there is little doubt as to the correctness of the general proportions. Relatively few Spaniards ever came to the Americas (North, Central, or South). Spanish colonization of the Americas was motivated by a desire for conquest[5] and was imposed upon the indigenous Indian population from above. In contrast to the English family settlement process, the Spanish expeditions were composed largely of the male nobility. At the time, Spain had little in the way of a middle class. Likewise, few of the lower class Spaniards settled in the New World. The nobles sought wealth and fame and had no intention of remaining permanently. Moreover, there were no succeeding waves of Spanish immigrants to fill the places of those who had returned to Europe. During the three hundred years following the Spanish exploration of the New World in the early sixteenth century, fewer than 300,000 Spaniards came to the Americas. Many of these died of disease, were killed in the numerous conflicts with the native Indian population, or, as indicated above, returned to Spain following their adventures. Accordingly, the concept of "la raza" ("the race") does not refer to any commonly agreed upon set of racial characteristics of the Chicano population itself. Indeed, the very concept "la raza" itself stems from the writings of the nineteenth century Mexican philosopher, José Vasconcelos, who set forth a mystical theory that it will be people [i.e., Mexicans] of mixed races ["la raza cosmica"] who will eventually dominate and rule the world. "La raza" came to mean a recognition of the fact that those of Mexican ancestry represent a commingling of the aggregate genes of New World Indians, Spaniards, Anglos, and, in a few instances, Negroes.

Not only are Chicanos racially distinct, but their experiences as an ethnic group frequently separate them from the majority Anglo population. The differences are manifested in language, family structure, religion, food, architecture, music, and literature preferences.[6] Ralph Guzman, the co-director of the Mexican-American Study Project at the University of California at Los Angeles, has commented:

The blacks have dealt with American society longer than we have. They can talk to white people easier. We still don't understand the white world, we still wrestle with what makes them laugh, what makes them angry, what this business is of looking people in the eye and shaking hands until they break. The Mexican American has resisted the acculturation process better than most immigrants. All groups try to resist but they are usually separated from their homeland and have not been successful. But Chicanos have been here all along and their culture is constantly fed by Mexico and the rest of Latin America.[7]

REGIONAL CONCENTRATION

The 1960 Census disclosed that 87 percent of all Chicanos lived in the five southwestern states. Eighty-two percent lived in California and Texas, which both had approximately the same size Chicano population (1.4 million people each). Hence, the general welfare of the Chicano population is intrinsically tied to developments within these two states. A special sample survey—the first of its kind—was conducted by the U.S. Bureau of the Census in November, 1969, of persons of *Spanish origin* (as distinct from the usual *Spanish surname* category). Although its sample was limited and there have been charges of undercount, the survey showed the continued dominance of those of Mexican origin in the southwestern states; namely, 84 percent of all people of Mexican origin in 1969 were found to reside in this five-state region.[8] Outside of the Southwest, the Chicano population is concentrated in rapidly growing communities in certain areas of Kansas, Nebraska, Illinois, Michigan, and Ohio.

The Southwest is uniquely different from the other sectors of the nation. Chicanos both contribute to and are affected by these regional features. The 1960 Census indicated that the Southwest population was more considerably urbanized (80 percent) than the nation as a whole (70 percent) and that the percent urban was approximately the same for Anglos (81 percent), nonwhites (80 percent), and Chicanos (79 percent) in the Southwest. The explanation for the high urban rate of all racial groups rests with the historic shortages of water over vast areas of land. As a result, people have tended to group together in an "oasis society."[9] The definition of "urban area," however, is one that includes all towns with a population of 2,500 or more. If one considers the proportion of population residing within Standard Metropolitan Statistical Areas (SMSA's), Chicanos had the lowest percentage (they were the least metropolitan) of the three major racial groupings. There are important differences among the residency patterns within the five-state region. In Texas, Colorado, and New Mexico, the Chicano population is highly concentrated in the poorest and least developed regions of these states. In California and Arizona, Chicanos are more dispersed. In 1960 Chicanos represented 11.8 percent of the population of the Southwest, whereas nonwhites totaled 9.3 percent for a nonAnglo population of 21.1 percent in the region. In passing, it should be noted that the nonwhite group in the Southwest is unique. It is only in Texas that nonwhite is predominantly black. In Arizona and New Mexico, American Indians dominate the group. Colorado has very few black citizens. In California, with its large Oriental population, 20 percent of the nonwhite population is nonblack.

RAPID GROWTH

The Chicano population is growing both relatively and absolutely. Between 1950 and 1960 (unfortunately the only two years for which comparable Census data are available), Chicanos accounted for 14.2 percent of the increase in population of the Southwest. Continued immigration (unrestricted until 1968, at which time a maximum of 120,000 a year from the Western hemisphere was imposed), inordinately high fertility rates (fertility rates for Chicanos are 70 percent higher than those of Anglos in the Southwest), and uncounted numbers of illegal entrants from across the 1,800-mile common border between Mexico and the United States all make certain the fact that the Chicano population in the decade 1960 to 1970 has sustained even greater gains in numbers.

It would be a mistake, however, to conclude that Chicanos are not predominately native Americans. In 1960, 54.8 percent of the Chicano population were native born of native-born parentage, with an additional 29.8 percent being native born to foreign-born parentage. Yet the fact remains that although only 15.4 percent were born in Mexico, this figure represents the largest foreign-born ethnic group now living in the United States.

NOTES

1. Carey McWilliams, *North from Mexico* (New York: Greenwood Press, 1968), p. 7.

2. "Remarks by Vincente T. Ximenes, Commissioner" (mimeographed material), press conference, Washington, D.C., May 28, 1970, p. 1.

3. William Greider, "A Family Fight Embitters Chicanos," *Washington Post,* May 25, 1969, p. B-3.

4. Jack D. Forbes, *Mexican-Americans: A Handbook for Educators* (Berkeley: Far West Laboratory for Educational Research and Development, :970).

5. McWilliams, *North from Mexico,* pp. 74–75.

6. For more detailed discussion of the racial and cultural characteristics of the Chicano population, see Leo Grebler *et al., The Mexican American People* (New York: Free Press, 1970), chapters 13-20.

7. Steven V. Roberts, "5% in U.S. Cite Spanish Origins," *New York Times,* April 18, 1971, p. 66.

8. "Persons of Spanish Origin in the United States: November 1969," *Current Population Reports,* series P-20, no. 213 (February, 1971), p. 4.

9. Fred H. Schmidt, *Spanish Surnamed Americans Employment in the Southwest* (Washington, D.C.: Government Printing Office, 1970), p. 50.

2

Special Considerations

HISTORICAL FACTORS

As with any racial and ethnic group, there are unique factors—past and present—which influence the Chicanos' current economic status. With blacks, one begins with slavery. With Chicanos,

. . . it is that the Southwest once represented an internal colonial empire to the United States. Those persons who first peopled the region, as well as their kinsmen who subsequently arrived were generally regarded as colonial subjects and were dealt with as such.[1]

The Southwest has approximated the experience in the Southeast in that it was settled and has remained heavily populated by Anglo natives of Anglo parentage. In 1960, 79.8 percent of the Southwest's population were Anglo. Moreover, a disproportionate number of the population are of Anglo-Saxon heritage and are Protestant. As a result, Chicanos have been racially, culturally, and religiously separated from the patterns of the majority population of the region.

Yet, although Anglos and Chicanos have had a long joint

history in the Southwest, it is also true that numerically Chicanos have become a sizable population only in the twentieth century. It is estimated that there were only about 100,000 Chicanos in the vast land area that became the Southwestern part of the United States at the termination of the Mexican-American War in 1848. During the remainder of the nineteenth century, the Immigration and Naturalization Service records show that fewer than 30,000 immigrants came to the United States. The subsequent Mexican immigration has come in two major spurts. The first was from 1911 through the early 1920s (roughly speaking, the time of the Mexican Revolutionary War) and the second from about 1955 through 1964. Since 1900, over 1.4 million people from Mexico have been legally admitted, and countless more have illegally entered.

STATISTICAL PROBLEMS

There are also several statistical problems that are crucial to any attempted analysis of Chicano employment—especially in rural areas. A large number of Chicanos have urban addresses but find employment in the agricultural sector of the economy. In 1960, 7 percent of the Chicano population living in urban areas were employed as farm laborers, as opposed to only .6 percent for Anglos and 2.1 percent for nonwhites. For migratory workers, cities are often used as home bases. In Texas, for example, the Texas Employment Commission estimates that fewer than 20 percent of the migratory workers in the state come from counties that are officially classified as "rural." Chicanos as a group are less urbanized than is readily apparent from statistics pertaining to domicile. Unlike the agricultural experience of blacks in the Southeast, there has been little need for Chicanos in the Southwest to reside on the land where they work.

Another serious problem that arises from Census data is that farm workers who are Mexican nationals but who are employed in the United States at the time of the decennial Census are included in the headcount. As a result, the socioeconomic status of the group appears to be lower than it actually is.[2] The inclusion is not a severe problem where large aggregates are concerned but it can result in a serious distortion where the population of Chicanos is small. At the time of the 1960 Census, there were 70,000 Mexican contract farm workers in the United States (33,000 in California, 24,000 in Texas, and the remainder scattered throughout the nation). The end of the bracero program (whereby Mexican nationals were legally allowed to do farmwork in the U.S.) in 1964 could mean that this problem will be lessened in the 1970 Census. It would follow that in part any improvement in the socioeconomic statistics for Chicanos between 1960 and 1970 would be illusory due to the presence of this poverty-stricken group in the former and its absence in the latter tabulations. By the same token, it should be noted that there has been a dramatic increase in the number of illegal entrants from Mexico since the end of the bracero program. It is unlikely that any official survey will adequately measure this group. As Fred Schmidt, the noted authority on Chicano labor market experience, has observed:

Those who enter the country without legal papers must live with uncertainty, no matter how long their residence here. Every representative of civil authority—whether welfare worker, employment service agent, Census enumerator, school official, or the like—becomes a potential threat to their tenuous status . . . . Given the uncertainties of their lot it is clear why such persons should wish to become "invisible" to all agents of authority. Their elusiveness contributes to the acknowledged undercount of the Census, suggesting that in the Southwest there is a shadow labor force whose number and characteristics are not fully reported in any official document.[3]

This growing number of illegal aliens means that the actual state of economic affairs among the Chicano labor force is far worse than the already gloomy figures portray and is most severe in the rural economy.

It is also important to realize that not all Chicanos have Spanish surnames. Some names have been changed to Anglo equivalents (i.e., Moreno to Brown, or Rey to King). Others have lost their Spanish surname through marriage. Because of this, many statistical studies that rely upon the 7,000 certified Spanish surnames used by the U.S. Census, as supplied originally by the U.S. Immigration and Naturalization Service, miss the actual dimensions of Chicano presence in local labor markets. Hence, it is recognized that there is significant "statistical slippage" of Chicanos in all official surveys.[4]

THE BORDER

Any discussion of special factors affecting the economic status of Chicanos must mention the unique feature of the Mexico-United States border. As it exists today, it was established by the Treaty of Guadalupe-Hidalgo in 1848 following the Mexican-American War and the Gadsden Purchase of 1853. The border's significance, however, transcends its geographical specifications:

The border itself is something of a fiction. It becomes real when some national policy of either of the nations wants to assert the fact of its existence, but most often it is a permeable thing, a membrane that joins rather than separates the nationally distinct communities.[5]

The critical role that the border assumes in a discussion of the economic welfare of rural Chicano workers will be subsequently explored in detail. For the moment, it is important to note a significant but often neglected effect that its presence has upon employment patterns on the United States side of the border: the border economy is heavily dependent upon the military as a source of livelihood. In 1960, a phenomenal total of 17.9 percent of all employed persons in the twenty-four counties of the four states that comprise the 1,800-mile border from Brownsville, Texas, to San Diego, California, were in the armed services.[6] The national average for 1960 was 2.6 percent of the total labor force in the military. With the growth of the armed services during the 1960s, it is likely that the percentage has risen. The effect of this inordinately heavy military presence is twofold: (1) it means that there is a large difference between the labor market statistics that pertain to the total labor force and those of the civilian labor force that is unlikely to be found in other regions of the nation, and (2) the local economy of the region has become heavily dependent upon military spending as a source of its well-being. In 1967, for example, one study of the border economy revealed that the Department of Defense spent $606 per capita in the border counties as opposed to a national figure of $290 per capita.[7] But the economic influence of government on the area transcends military considerations. When all forms of federal funds are considered, $1,033 was spent per capita in the border area in 1967 as opposed to a national average of $853.[8] As for employment, all levels of government (federal, state, and local) accounted for 21 percent of the civilian labor force in 1967.[9] Thus, there is no doubt that government is the major employer in the region where Chicanos are most numerous. The degree to which Chicanos are government employees remains to be determined by future research. In passing, it is worthy to note that San Antonio, which is *not* located in a border county, has in relative terms the highest proportion of Chicanos (41 percent of the SMSA have Spanish surnames; perhaps 10 percent *more* actually are Chicanos) of any major city or SMSA in the nation and is also heavily dependent upon the military for its well-being. There are four major military bases in the San Antonio area plus a world-famous military hospital complex for the treatment of burns. It was of no small consequence when U.S. Congressman Henry B. Gonzales from San Antonio quipped that "the Anglos can have the Alamo as long as we control Kelly Field"[10] (Kelly Field is the largest single employer in the city).

INCIDENCE OF POVERTY

The inordinately high incidence of poverty is one of the most serious problems confronting Chicanos. In 1960, 32.8 percent of the Chicano population in the Southwest were officially classified as being poor (1,082,000 persons in families).[11] The 1960 figures underestimated the actual poverty population because they are for family people only—excluding persons living as individuals. For Chicanos, the only racial group in the United States in which the number of males exceeds the number of females in the population, the exclusion was serious. In rural areas, where the ratio of males to females was 1.3 to 1 in 1960, the category of unrelated individuals is an extremely important index of group welfare.

By 1970, the absolute number of Chicanos in the Southwest living in the official state of poverty was 1,283,000 persons in families.[12] Thus, over the prosperous decade of the 1960s, the net absolute change in the Chicano poverty population for the region was an *increase* of 101,000 people. In relative terms, the percentage of all Chicano family persons living in poverty declined slightly to 29.4 percent of the total. Figures for unrelated individuals are available for 1970. They disclose that in the Southwest 34.5 percent (or 53,000 people) of the Chicanos who were so classified were living in poverty.[13] Thus, with almost 1 out of every 3 Chicanos "officially" living in a state of poverty and countless thousands more just barely over the statistically defined threshold, poverty is an ongoing and pervasive fact of Chicano life in the United States.

LOW EDUCATIONAL ATTAINMENT

In addition to a high incidence of poverty, an extremely low level of educational attainment is a characteristic of the Chicano population. In 1960, the Census reported that for persons fourteen years and over in the Southwest the median level years of school completion was 12.0 for Anglos, 9.7 for nonwhites, and 8.1 for Chicanos. The question of educational quality, of course, is even more important, especially for children of migratory workers, and it is left moot by the statistics. The lowest state median was in Texas with 4.8 years of education for Chicanos over twenty-five years of age, and the highest was California with 8.6 years. With the exception of the American Indian, no major racial group in America produces fewer high school graduates. In addition, only 6 percent of the Chicano population had any college training, compared to 12 percent for nonwhites and 25 percent for Anglos. The functional illiteracy rate (0-4 years of schooling) for Chicanos of 27.6 percent in 1960 was seven times that of Anglos and twice that of blacks.

In 1966, the final report of a commission established under the terms of the Civil Rights Act of 1964 to survey the equality of educational opportunity in America was made public. The report, known popularly as the Coleman Report, revealed that, when compared to standardized achievement of Anglos in the metropolitan Northeast, Chicanos fell increasingly behind the longer they remained in school. The differential in grades in verbal ability was 2.0 years at the end of the sixth grade, 2.3 years at the end of the ninth

15

grade, and 3.5 years at the end of the twelfth grade; in reading comprehension, it was 2.4 years at the end of the sixth grade, 2.6 years at the end of the ninth grade, and 3.3 years at the end of the twelfth grade; in mathematical achievement, it was 2.2 years at the end of the sixth grade, 2.6 years at the end of the ninth grade, and 4.1 years at the end of the twelfth grade.[14] Although these tests made no pretense of being culturally fair, it was alleged that their consent measured knowledge which many employers feel is "increasingly important for success in our society."[15]

The previously mentioned 1969 study of persons of Spanish origin indicated a trend toward a bimodal distribution with respect to educational experience within the Mexican origin group. There were significant differences in the educational attainment of persons thirty-five years and over from those persons twenty-five to thirty-four years. The median level for the former was 7.3 years; for the latter, it was 10.8 years. These figures indicate that although improvements are occurring, the Mexican origin group was still significantly below (for both the over thirty-five and the twenty-five to thirty-four group) the comparable educational attainment medians for the entire Spanish origin grouping (11.7 years and 8.5 years respectively). It is also certain that the Chicano figures remain below those of the Anglos and nonwhites even if allowances are made for differences between young and older experiences.

Between 1971 and 1972, the U.S. Commission on Civil Rights released three exhaustive reports of its investigations of Chicano educational experience in the Southwest. In its evaluation, the commission concluded that relative to their Anglo student counterparts "their school holding power is lower; their reading achievement is poorer; their repetition of grades is more frequent; and they participate in extracurricular activities to a lesser degree."[16] The commission found that Chicanos were significantly isolated in de facto segregated schools and that they suffered severely from "cultural exclusion" with respect to curriculum, textbooks, and instructional methods.[17] To enhance the retention power of the schools, the commission recommended extensive reliance upon bilingual education and the addition of course materials which relate the Chicano heritage and contribution to the cultural development of the region.

The factor most often cited as the cause for the relatively unfavorable educational performance of Chicanos is the language issue. In 1969, it was reported that in 47.3 percent of the families of Mexican origin, Spanish was the language usually spoken in the home. It is likely that the incidence of this is higher in rural than in urban areas. The limited exposure that many Chicano youngsters have to English often becomes an issue of conflict when the youths begin school. Enrique Hank Lopez, a consultant to the Ford Foundation, has capsuled the issue:

Many of us are not really bilingual but schizolingual. We actually speak an amalgam of English and Spanish that creates special problems in education. For every human being, the greatest period of learning is from birth to age 5 and for the Chicano child that learning is taking place in this schizolingual amalgam, which is mostly Spanish. This is the child's principal cognitive tool but the day he enters school it is snatched away from him. You may as well perform a partial lobotomy on him. He's so severely traumatized at a crucial period in kindergarten. When he's forbidden to talk his own language, he gets a terrific sense of inferiority and guilt. He begins to dislike himself and his parents and everyone else.[18]

Nonetheless, one of the most characteristic aspects of the labor market experience of Chicanos is the group's ability to demonstrate higher earnings than any other nonAnglo group at comparable levels of educational attainment. Rela-

17

tive to Anglos, however, Chicanos have not received equivalent returns.[19]

NOTES

1. Fred H. Schmidt, *Spanish Surnamed Americans Employment in the Southwest* (Washington, D.C.: Government Printing Office, 1970), p. 7.

2. Leo Grebler *et al., The Mexican American People* (New York: Free Press, 1970), p. 604.

3. Fred H. Schmidt, "The Current Economic Condition of the Mexican-American," a paper presented to the Conference on Economic and Educational Perspectives of the Mexican-American, Aspen, Colo., August 28, 1972, p. 5.

4. Grebler, *Mexican-American,* p. 604.

5. Schmidt, *Spanish Surnamed Americans,* p. 61.

6. Ibid., p. 47.

7. David S. North, *The Border Crossers: People Who Live in Mexico and Work in the United States* (Washington, D.C.: Trans Century Corporation, 1970), p. 38.

8. Ibid.

9. Ibid., p. 37.

10. William Grieder, "A Family Fight Embitters Chicanos," *Washington Post* (May 25, 1969), p. B-5.

11. Grebler, *Mexican American,* p. 198.

12. U.S. Bureau of the Census, "Characteristics of the Low-Income Population, 1970," Current Population Reports, series P-60, no. 81 (Washington, D.C.: U.S. Government Printing Office, 1971), p. 50.

13. Ibid.

14. *Equality of Educational Opportunity* (Washington, D.C.: U.S. Department of Health, Education, and Welfare, 1966), pp. 274–75. This report is more popularly known as the Coleman Report for its chairman, James S. Coleman.

15. Ibid., p. 273.

16. U.S. Commission on Civil Rights, *The Unfinished Education,* rept. 2 of the Mexican American Educational Series, October, 1971 (Washington, D.C.: U.S. Government Printing Office, 1971), pp. 41–42.

17. In addition to the above cited report, the Civil Rights Commission's findings are also presented in *Ethnic Isolation of Mexican Americans in the Public Schools of the Southwest,* Report 1, April 1971, and *The Excluded Student,* Rept. 3, May, 1972, which are the remaining volumes in the series.

18. Steven V. Roberts, "5% in U.S. Cite Spanish Origins," *New York Times* (August 18, 1971), p. 66.

19. Walter Fogel, "The Effect of Low Educational Attainment on Incomes: A Comparative Study of Selected Ethnic Groups," *The Journal of Human Resources,* vol. 1, no. 2 (Fall 1966), pp. 22–40. Also see Vernon M. Briggs, Jr., *Negro Employment in the South: The Houston Labor Market* (Washington, D.C.: U.S. Government Printing Office, 1971), chap. 2. Chicano income and employment records are consistently more favorable than those for blacks despite the fact that the black educational attainment median was three years higher than that of Chicanos.

3

The Rural Labor Market of the Southwest

Control of the vast land areas in the Southwest has always been an issue for dispute. The Indians fought each other; the early Spanish settlers fought the Indians; the Mexicans fought the Anglos; the Anglos fought the remaining Indians and then fought among themselves. The range wars between the farmers and the ranchers, the bitter fighting between the sheep herders and the cattlemen, and the violent struggle between labor and management in the mining areas were all part of the settlement process. To this day, there remain many conflicts over the legal ownership and use of land. The Alianza movement in New Mexico, for example, which began under the leadership of Reis Lopez Tijerina in 1962, has centered over the validity of Spanish land grants guaranteed under the 1848 Treaty of Guadalupe-Hidalgo. In the same dispute, American Indians have filed counterclaims challenging the rights of the Spanish king to have given title to this same land to the early Spanish settlers in the first place.

Focusing upon the Anglos and the Chicanos, there has been much controversy over just how the Anglos acquired the land the Chicanos now depend upon as their source of employment. Ambiguity, violence, and skullduggery were all involved. The amount of this is uncertain, but the result is undebatable.

In the development of the region, it is likely that economics became as much the villain as the foibles of human greed or of racial bigotry. Agriculture, ranching, and mining dominated the industrial base of the region throughout its early history and remain significant to this day. In the early days, these industries were highly dependent on labor and became magnets for migrant laborers. They were also heavily capitalized industries, which meant that Eastern money and absentee ownership became the rule and is still the pattern today.

In terms of numbers, it is agriculture that has been the mainstay of the rural economy for Chicanos. The vast majority of the Mexicans who migrated into the Southwest in the twentieth century came from a rural agricultural background. Many of the illegal aliens continue to follow this route. Speaking little English and having few skills to offer an urban labor market, most of these immigrants and aliens have become trapped in working for America's most exploitive industry.

LIMITED OWNERSHIP OPPORTUNITIES

The sheer scale of agricultural operations in the Southwest has meant that few Chicano immigrants have had the opportunity to become farm or ranch owners themselves. The only notable exception to this pattern is the Chicano settlement in northern New Mexico which dates back to the seventeenth century and which was largely isolated from regional development until the 1940s. For this small enclave, the major challenge for land ownership to the Chicano community has come from the incorporation by the federal government of their communal grazing lands into the National Forest System.

Land ownership in the Southwest has always been the domain of large business enterprises with immense financial capabilities. This historic characteristic of bigness has been exacerbated in recent years by the entry into the industry through vertical mergers of conglomerate corporations such as Tenneco, Standard Oil, Kaiser Aluminum, and the Southern Pacific Railroad. To the degree that medium-sized to large-sized farms (those with annual sales between $20,000 and $500,000) exist in the region, they are increasingly threatened by a financial and business organization revolution. The traditional functions of the food supply system are being abandoned, altered, combined, and coordinated by giant multi-industrial corporations. Although the consolidation movement is a nationwide phenomenon, it is galloping at its most rapid pace in California. California is the nation's largest agricultural producer. It alone produces 40 percent of the nation's vegetables, nuts, and fruits; moreover, it provides at least 90 percent of the country's supply of 15 crops and leads the nation in the production of an additional 25. Approximately 42 percent of the farmworkers in California are Chicanos, and the implications both as individuals or a group are ominous. For they—as well as others who live in the rural areas of the Southwest—who have low or moderate incomes can neither enter nor influence the dominant industry in their local economies.

The impact of agribusiness in the Southwest has been succinctly captured by the following passage:

It has been said that the strings of California's $3.6 billion-a-year agribusiness are pulled from the redwood paneled offices on San Francisco's Montgomery Street, the Wall Street of the West. In addition to growers, packers, processors, middlemen, and distributors, agribusiness embraces allied enterprises such as banks (the Bank of America, the world's largest, is the prime financier of California farms), shipping and transportation companies, land companies (Kern County Land Company for all practical purposes *is* Kern County), and utilities, plus other large corporations which have a stake in the prosperity of the field-to-table process.

The anatomy of this "giant octopus," as one packing company executive put it, can be seen by studying the interlocking directorships of the agribusiness corporations. Packing executives sit on the boards of directors of banks and land companies. Bankers who trade in farm loans proliferate on the boards of packing and land companies. Realty executives who deal in farm acreage sit on the boards of shipping and packing companies. The labyrinth goes on and on.

As a group, agribusiness executives are hardheaded and dollar-oriented, which is by way of saying they are not much different from executives in other fields. The tremendous technological advances of agriculture are all to their credit, but where they differ from executives in other fields is in their concept of their responsibility to human beings.[1]

For Chicanos, the combination of these factors has meant that it is virtually impossible to convert hard work into personal gain.[2] There have been scant opportunities for occupational advancement since most agricultural jobs are of a dead-end variety.

Except for the Depression years of the 1930s, it was not until 1965 that there was any effort made to control the flow of Mexican immigrants into the industry's labor pool. The resulting low wage scale, combined with highly seasonal opportunities to work, meant that farm worker income has hovered at the subsistence level. The 1960 Census disclosed that 52.2 percent of the Chicano families living in rural areas had an income below $3,000 a year (14.2 percent had an annual family income of below $1,000).[3] One study summarized the situation this way:

The Spanish-speaking work more days for less pay and have a higher rate of unemployment than other farm workers. In 1960, the average income of a Spanish-speaking farm worker in the Southwest was $1,256 for 183 days of work.[4]

Another characteristic of southwestern agricultural employment that affects Chicanos is that the crops are not usually price supported. Fresh fruits and vegetables are the major sources of employment opportunities. Hence, these products are more subject to price fluctuations than are the major agricultural staples in the Southeast, cotton and tobacco. With respect to minority employment patterns in the United States, it is significant to note that blacks employed in agriculture are almost exclusively involved in the cultivation, preharvest, and harvest of federally price supported commodities; Chicanos are not.

THE SIGNIFICANCE OF EXISTING TRENDS

To this point the discussion has focused upon agriculture as it impinges upon the economic life of the Chicano community. For Anglos, and sometimes for blacks, such a focus can be a source of error. For often much of the rural labor force is not employed in agriculture but rather in the vast array of jobs associated with small towns, recreation, leisure, and government employment. Although there are only a few of these jobs in each community in the collective rural economy they represent a substantial total. This is decidedly *not* the case for Chicanos. Agriculture is the dominant source of employment and income for most Chicanos who reside in the rural Southwest. (See tables 2 and 3.) It should be recalled that an additional 7.4 percent of the *urban* Chicano labor force were also employed in agriculture in 1960 (41,000 urban males were farm laborers, and 4,000 urban males were farmers and farm managers).

The trends in rural southwestern labor markets reveal extensive mechanization, growing farm sizes, and increasing income for a few corporations but massive underemployment and pervasive poverty for many people. The limited occupational horizons confronting the Chicanos of the region have been aptly described as constituting a "caste system."[5] It is virtually impossible for Chicanos to surmount the prevailing barriers in order to secure advancement opportunities.

Yet, the pitiful irony of the situation is that the public policy of the United States government and of the state governments of the region has done more to compound and to perpetuate the misery of the rural Chicano labor force than it has to alleviate their suffering and to resolve their predicament. Specifically, the adverse policies can be grouped into two categories: (1) those that uniquely pertain to the supply

Table 2. Industrial employment patterns of Spanish-surnamed people in the rural southwest, 1960

Industry	Thousands of people	Percentage
Agirculture, forestry, and fisheries	101	50.2
Mining	5	2.5
Construction	11	5.5
Manufacturing	15	7.6
Transportation, communication, and utilities	9	4.3
Wholesale and retail trade	21	10.4
Finance, insurance, and real estate	1	.6
Personal services	23	11.2
Government	5	2.7
Not reported	10	5.0
Total	201	100.0

SOURCE: U.S. Census of 1960 as reported in Olen E. Leonard and Helen W. Johnson, *Low-Income Families in the Spanish-Surname Population of the Southwest* (Washington, D.C.: U.S. Department of Agriculture, 1967), Agricultural Economic Rept. no. 112, p. 17.

Table 3. Occupational patterns of Spanish-surnamed males in the rural southwest, 1960

Occupation	Thousands of males	Percentage
Professional, technical managers, and officials	7	4.2
Farmers and farm managers	13	7.6
Clerical and sales	5	2.8
Craftsmen and operators	36	21.7
Service workers	5	3.2
Farm laborers	76	45.5
Laborers (except farm and mine)	16	9.7
Not reported	9	5.3
Total	167	100.0

SOURCE: U.S. Census of 1960 as reported in Olen E. Leonard and Helen W. Johnson, *Low-Income Families in the Spanish-Surname Population of the Southwest* (Washington, D.C.: U.S. Department of Agriculture, 1967), Agricultural Economic Rept. no. 112, p. 17.

of Chicano workers and (2) those that relate to the general state of agricultural employment conditions. Because of the importance of these issues, each will be dealt with in the following two chapters.

NOTES

1. Steve Allen, "Agribusiness: The Corporate Sector," *The Ground is Our Table* (Garden City: Doubleday and Company, Inc., 1966), p. 46 [Emphasis is in the original].

2. Leo Grebler et al., *The Mexican-American People* (New York: Free Press, 1970), p. 90.

3. Olen E. Leonard and Helen W. Johnson, *Low-Income Families in the Spanish-Surname Population of the Southwest* (Washington, D.C.: U.S. Department of Agriculture, 1967), Agricultural Economic Rept. no. 112, p. 12.

4. Lawrence B. Glick, "The Right to Equal Opportunity," ed. Julian Samora, *La Raza: Forgotten Americans* (South Bend: University of Notre Dame, 1966), p 100.

5. Grebler, *Mexican American*, pp. 8–9.

4

Labor Supply and Public Policy

The noted authority on Chicano life in the United States, the late George I. Sánchez, wrote:

The most serious threats to an effective program of acculturation in the Southwest have been the population movements from Mexico: first by illegal aliens, the so-called "wetbacks," then by the bracero program, and finally by the commuters. . . . Time and again, just as we have been on the verge of cutting our bicultural problems to manageable proportions, uncontrolled mass migrations from Mexico have erased the gains and accentuated the cultural indigestion.[1]

Immigration from Mexico has since the 1920s centered upon agricultural labor conditions in the United States. As indicated earlier, Chicanos have been inordinately concentrated in agricultural employment in the Southwest. In 1960, for example, Census data disclosed that 20 percent of all Spanish-speaking wage earners worked at least sometime in agriculture.[2] For Chicanos, the percentage is undoubtedly higher since the term Spanish-speaking embraces a number of groups other than Chicanos who, as a rule, do not seek employment in the agricultural sector.[3]

Most of the immigrants have come from rural areas of Mexico, which means they have had a rural culture and tradition. The original impetus was the push of the Mexican Revolution and the simultaneous pull of industrial needs of the United States during World War I. Many Anglos were drafted and, with immigration from Europe stopped for the first time in the nation's history, a new agricultural labor force was needed in the Southwest. After the war, many former agricultural workers did not return to the rural areas. Thus, the demand for Mexicans remained strong, and, because they were not covered by the quotas imposed by the National Origins Act of 1924, the supply responded in the predicted manner. With no new immigrant group seeking to fill the unskilled and semiskilled jobs of the Southwest, the outflow from Mexico served to keep wages in these occupations at the "existence level" (to use one of Cesar Chavez's terms). Until the Depression hit, Mexicans were welcomed. The displaced Anglos from the dust bowl areas then became the cheap labor supply, and many Chicanos were forcibly repatriated to Mexico. This period marked the height of suppressive attitudes of the Anglo community toward Chicano citizens. U.S. Congressman John C. Box of Texas, who had lost out in an earlier effort to have Mexicans included under the restrictive racial quotas of the Immigration Act of 1924, scornfully and slanderously described Mexicans during this period as "a mixture of Mediterranean blooded Spanish peasants with low grade Indians who did not fight to extinction but submitted and multiplied as serfs."[4] The Hoover administration initiated the first effort of the United States to regulate the flow of immigrants from south of the border.

THE BRACERO PROGRAM

Not until World War II were Mexican farmworkers again needed. Originally they did not come in large numbers for fear of the draft and because the Mexican economy was prospering. A formal arrangement was consummated between the governments of the United States and Mexico in 1942 (Public Law 45) that provided guarantees on working conditions and steady employment for short periods of seasonal farm work. The Mexican labor program, better known as the bracero program, was initiated as a war emergency measure. The formal statutory program lasted until 1947. Under its terms, braceros were not allowed to be sent into Texas because of the wide-spread discriminatory treatment of Chicanos.[5] The binational agreement ended December 31, 1947; however it continued informally—but unregulated—until 1951 when it was reconstituted formally as Public Law 78 and provided for the inclusion of Texas. Public Law 78 was strongly supported by growers under the cloak of labor shortages induced by the Korean conflict. Table 4 indicates the magnitude of the program. Obviously, its peak usage was *after* the Korean War years. The U.S. Department of Labor terminated the program as of December 31, 1964. The operation of this controversial program served to displace many native Chicanos from the rural labor market. The proportion of Chicanos living in urban areas increased sharply from 66.4 percent in 1950 to 79.1 percent in 1960. The bracero was a prime contributor to the urban movement. It is also worthy to repeat that there has been a sharp rise in illegal entrants from Mexico since the end of the program in 1964 with the probable effect of further pressure being exerted upon rural Chicanos to move to the cities.

There were numerous accounts of grower favoritism of braceros to the detriment of native Chicanos. The bracero program represents a classic example of how institutionally imposed rules can affect the exchange process in rural labor markets. The relative wage of agricultural workers to manufacturing workers declined sharply during this period. Growers

29

Table 4. A Comparison of annual numbers of Mexican braceros and deported Mexican Nationals, 1948–1971

Year	Mexican braceros	Illegal entrants, deported to Mexico
1948	35,345	193,852
1949	107,000	289,400
1950	67,500	469,581
1951	192,000	510,355
1952	197,100	531,719
1953	201,380	839,149
1954	309,033	1,035,282
1955	398,650	165,186
1956	445,197	58,792
1957	436,049	45,640
1958	432,857	45,164
1959	437,643	42,732
1960	315,846	39,750
1961	291,420	39,860
1962	194,978	41,200
1963	186,865	51,230
1964	177,736	41,589
1965	20,286	48,948
1966	8,647	89,683
1967	7,703	107,695
1968	0	142,520
1969	0	189,572
1970	0	265,539
1971	0	348,000

SOURCE: U.S. Department of Labor and the Immigration and Naturalization Service of the U.S. Department of Justice.

claimed that if the program were abandoned a severe labor shortage would ensue. Yet if wages are artificially held at low relative positions, the fear of a domestic labor shortage can hardly be conceived of as a market phenomenon that justifies the existence of the program. The shortage, should it materialize, would be manmade. The increases in wages since the end of the program have clearly shown that domestic labor is available if the monetary inducements are in any way competitive with alternative opportunities.

In reality, the bracero program can only be understood in the context of a prolonged series of government-sanctioned endeavors designed to guarantee many employers in the Southwest what is a perfectly elastic supply of labor—a seemingly infinite number of available workers at a given wage rate. The harshest aspect of the bracero program, however, was the symbolic indifference it manifested to the Chicano population:

> Imagine, if you will, Big Steel importing as the nucleus of its work force Polish steelworkers willing to work at little more than Iron Curtain wages. Imagine the electronics industry bringing in cadres of patient Japanese assembly-line workers at subpar Oriental wages. Imagine the various manufacturing and construction industries importing in wholesale lots of unskilled and semi-skilled workers from impoverished countries, eager to toil for a pittance. All of this with the stamp of approval—and helping hand—of the United States government.[6]

ILLEGAL ENTRANTS

The bracero program is formally a thing of the past. The problem of illegal entrants was and continues to be an issue. Actual statistics as to numbers of illegal entrants are, of course, unattainable. Figures are available only for those apprehended and deported back to Mexico by the Immigration and Naturalization Service (INS) of the U.S. Department of Justice. As shown in table 4, there has been a dramatic increase in the number of deportations to Mexico beginning with the termination of the bracero program in 1965. It is reliably estimated that for every one illegal entrant that is deported, another has gone undetected and is presently at work.[7] Testifying before a congressional committee in 1971, the commissioner of the INS commented ominously about the rate of increase in illegal entrants along the southern border:

The trend will be upward. The Mexican-U.S. border situation has grown progressively worse. The job market in Mexico is not keeping pace with the population increase, the second largest in the world. The higher wage in the United States is ever present and border violations continue to mount.[8]

The population explosion in Mexico, the high Mexican unemployment rate (especially among youth), the extreme difference in wage rates and income levels between the two nations, memories of earnings under the old bracero program, and just plain economic desperation have been cited as explanations in the various reports on the subject. The illegal entrant traffic was not affected by the bracero program. In fact, as always, many growers and ranchers could save money by knowingly employing illegal entrants. For there were controls placed on the treatment of braceros which entailed expenditures of both money and time. In the matter of housing, for instance, the braceros were (and most illegal entrants are) single men, whereas the domestic migrants are often families whose costs for housing are higher. For American labor, the illegal entrants have served to depress wages and working conditions.

Presently the immigration statutes contain the so-called Texas proviso. Adopted originally as a compromise to the Texas congressional delegation, the proviso states that the types of services that employers furnish employees, such as housing, feeding, and transporting, shall not count as an illegal act of harboring illegal immigrants. Clearly, the intent of the section is to render employers immune from prosecution if they hire illegal entrants. To this end, the exemption has accomplished its objective. Until it is made illegal, the practice will continue. As it stands, it is a game of chance for the illegal worker. If he is caught, he is deported; if not, he has a job that is often better than the alternatives available in Mexico. For the businessman, there is no risk of loss with only gains to be had from tapping a cheap source of labor.

The problem of illegal entrants for the 1970s upon Chicano welfare cannot be overstated. In 1954, conditions became severe enough to warrant the launching of Operation Wetback by the federal government. As shown in table 4, a record number of people were deported in that year, although many came back to the United States under the now defunct bracero program. Illegal entrants are rapidly increasing. As most are single men, extremely poor, and know only farm labor, they are a real threat to Chicanos who seek employment in the agricultural and nonfarm rural economy. A 1970 study, which recommended that a new Operation Wetback program be launched (but hopefully with a less offensive title), summed up the prevailing situation as follows:

> If no stepped-up actions, and sensible ones, are taken, we will shortly be back in the situation we had in the fifties when labor markets along the border and inland were flooded with these hapless and rightless workers.[9]

Illegal entrants are both the victims themselves and the perpetrators of suffering to others in the rural economy of the Southwest.

THE COMMUTERS

No discussion of institutionally manipulated labor supply factors and Chicano labor market experience would be complete without mention of its most unique phenomenon: the commuters. In his definitive study of border labor problems, David S. North has aptly said that "the commuter is this generation's bracero."[10] There are people who live in Mexico but work in the United States. They may be Mexican nationals or United States citizens, including those who have been naturalized. Principally, there are two groups involved. One is commonly known as "green-carders," so named for the original color of the cards used to cross the border. They have been legally admitted as immigrants and are free to live and work anywhere in the United States. The second group are "white-carders," similarly named for the color of their border-crossing cards. They are classified as legal visitors, who supposedly can stay in the United States for only seventy-two hours at a time within a 150 mile radius of the border. White-carders are technically forbidden to be employed while "visiting" this country—but it is an accepted fact that the law is honored largely in its breach.[11] Similarly, a court decision acknowledged it to be "amiable fiction" that many green-carders actually reside in the United States. For a substantial number, false addresses such as only a postal mail box number or the home of a relative are common, while actually these workers live in Mexico.

Beginning with the Immigration Act of 1952, the secretary of labor was granted the authority to block entry of immigrants from Mexico if their presence would endanger prevailing American labor standards. The Immigration Act of 1965 added to the authority of the Department of Labor. It set forth a requirement that job seekers must also receive a labor certification stating that a shortage of workers exists in the applicant's particular occupation and that his employment will not affect prevailing wages and working conditions in an adverse manner. The certification procedure became effective July 1, 1968. The certification is made *only once*—at the time of *initial* application as an immigrant.

Yet less one become too excited about the regulatory effectiveness of the labor certification process, it should be noted that the entire process is fraught with loopholes. Only one of every 13 members of the alien work force is subject to labor certification. In his definitive investigation of the effectiveness of the procedure, North concluded that

we question the overall significance of a fairly stringent procedure which covers such a tiny portion of the problem. It might be compared to building a massive dam which reached only one-thirteenth of the way across the Mississippi.[12]

In addition to labor certification, there are a number of other formalities involved in the process of securing a green card. To obtain a visa, a good conduct statement must be obtained from Mexican police officials; a birth certificate and a Mexican passport are required; an interview with an American consular official is needed to determine if the applicant is of good moral caliber and unlikely to become a public charge. A medical examination is necessary. If the visa is granted and labor certification approved, the Immigration and Naturalization Service can issue a green card, Form 151. From what little data are available, it is the fear of becoming a public charge that is the major reason for denial of entry to the many who apply for the visa.[13] To secure a white card, the consular decision on such matters is not required.

There are ways of circumventing the restrictions for obtaining a green card. All family members of anyone who holds a green card are eligible for American citizenship upon application. Any relative of an adult American citizen is also eligible, and these people are exempt from the 120,000 quota limitation imposed in 1968. Moreover, if a Mexican citizen has a baby while in the United States, the child's birth gives it citizenship which then entitles all relatives of the child to claim citizenship. A pregnant woman who obtains a border-crossing card (a white card) and who gives birth in the United States then can secure entry for herself and all other family members.

Once a green card is obtained, the holder is free to come and to go as long as no absence from the United States exceeds one year in duration or he doesn't become unemployed for over six months. In theory, the green-carder is identical to any other resident immigrant; in fact, this is not the case. Green-carders are not required to live in the United States; they must be employed to retain their status; they cannot serve as strikebreakers; and they cannot count the time that they live in foreign countries toward the years needed to become an American citizen. In practice, however, most of these distinctions are not significant. The requirement that one not be unemployed for more than six months is not enforced on the southern border even though it *is* enforced on the Canadian border; the antistrikebreaker rule is so easily circumvented that it is essentially meaningless; and many green-carders are simply not interested in becoming American citizens.

It is only in a technical sense that green-carders resemble other resident immigrants. A thorough 1970 study of green-carders revealed that few of them actually register for the draft, even though they are required to do so.[14] Those that do register are almost always classified as I-Y or IV-F.[15] The reason for the large number of I-Y classifications is that the mental test is given only in English. It is only in Puerto Rico that the draftee is given a choice of taking the test in Spanish or English. The same study disclosed that most green-carders seldom pay Federal income taxes either.[16] Green-carders simply claim a sufficient number of deductions to assure that no taxes are due. The Internal Revenue Service (IRS) is not permitted to cross the Mexican border to check the validity of deduction claims. Moreover, the Immigration and Naturalization Service does not use Social Security numbers for identification purposes, so their records are of little use to IRS officials. If green cards were renewable annually rather than being permanent documents, this loophole could be closed. The fact that wages of domestics and of farm-workers are not subject to withholding tax provisions makes the tax situation even more absurd. As for white-carders, they are nonresident aliens who are *not* supposed to hold jobs. Hence, there can be no collection of taxes unless the entire masquerade is exposed.

Precisely how many commuters of either the green or white card variety there are is a mystery. A 1969 report claimed that "approximately 70,000 persons cross the Mexico border *daily* to work in the United States."[17] Of these, 20,000 were U.S. citizens living in Mexico, and 50,000 were Mexican immigrants who had valid immigration documents but who lived in Mexico while working in the United States. A 1968 report by the U.S. Commission on Civil Rights placed the *total number* of green card holders at 650,000 with an additional 1,250,000 white card holders.[18] The fact that there are no reliable data pertaining to the precise numbers of characteristics of these commuters has been labeled "astonishing" in the comprehensive 1970 report of the Mexican American Study Project at the University of California at Los Angeles.[19]

As mentioned earlier, a restriction was placed on the employment of green-carders in 1967 which bars them from employment at locations at which there is a certified (by the secretary of labor) labor dispute. The effect of the anti-strikebreaker amendment is essentially nullified by the fact that employers usually have ample time after a dispute occurs to employ green-carders before it is officially certified.[20] Because there is no notation made as to when green-carders cross the border, it is impossible to tell whether the possessor of the card was hired before or after a strike was called. Furthermore, a strike situation in the United States differs markedly from that of Mexico. In Mexico, it is against the law for a plant to operate if a strike is called; this is not the case in the United States. American enterprises that are struck may elect to keep open if they can find workers willing to cross picket lines. In the agricultural industry, this is the usual practice. Consequently, not all green-carders and others coming from Mexico fully understand this phenomenon. In other instances, studies have shown that some green-carders fear that their card could be revoked should they participate in a strike, some are simply not interested in being unionized, and still others are not reachable by union organizers and strikers because employers transport them from the actual border fence directly to the job site.

Strangely, the commuter system functions without a statutory base. Prior to 1927, there were no formalities involved in crossing the border. Commuting workers were viewed as "alien visitors." On April 1, 1927, however, the Immigration and Naturalization Service ruled that such individuals were now to be considered as immigrants who required a visa to be so classified. The INS decision was upheld by the Supreme Court in 1929 (*Karuth* vs. *Albro*) with the famous interpretation that "employment equals residence," thereby avoiding the permanent residency requirement of the immigration statutes. The question of actual residence, therefore, became a moot point insofar as the INS was concerned. For contemporary justification, the perpetuation of the system is derived from a Board of Immigration Appeals decision in 1958:

> The commuter situation does not fit into any precise category found in the immigration statutes. The status is an artificial one, predicated upon good international relations maintained and cherished between friendly neighbors.[21]

The gist of the result is this:

> The U.S. worker who competes with the traffic of workers from Mexico is caught in a situation where he pays a substantial part of what the Secretary of State regards as a form of foreign aid to a neighboring nation.[22]

The commuters themselves are often exploited.[23] They do *not* receive any of the legal protection extended earlier to braceros. For example, they are not required to be paid the prevailing wage; they are usually not provided transportation between jobs; and they are not guaranteed a certain number of days of work.

Of course, not all commuters work in agriculture. Many work in low wage garment industries and retail shops on the U.S. side of the border. Nonetheless, one estimate is that 60 percent or more of all commuters entering California and Arizona are farmworkers; in Texas, the figure was listed as 18 percent.[24] Yet their presence has had its effect on both the border economy and the character of rural employment for Chicanos living in the region. As the U.S. Civil Rights Commission found:

> The impact of the commuter is particularly acute in agriculture where mechanization is rapidly reducing job opportunities. Due to the high concentration of farms along the border and the fact that commuters often work in the lowest skilled, lowest paid jobs, farm workers, who are already underpaid, are the first to suffer competition from the commuter. Furthermore, the use of commuters as strikebreakers is especially damaging to this group's organizational struggles.[25]

In addition, the impact of commuters has forced many Chicanos who are permanent residents of the United States and who must survive in its climate of higher cost of living into the migratory worker stream. The Civil Rights Commission reported that the lack of jobs in south Texas forced 88,700 farmworkers in 1968 to migrate elsewhere to find employment while commuters easily find jobs in the local economy. One-half of the Texas migrant workers come from the four counties of the lower Rio Grande valley. The importance of the welfare of migratory workers to a study of rural poverty cannot be overstressed. In fact, migratory agricultural work is the single largest occupational category for the Chicano labor force. The relationship of the commuter problem to migratory workers has been summarized in the testimony of Manuel Ramirez, a VISTA staff member assigned to Laredo, Texas before the Civil Rights Commission:

These people see the problem of the commuter as a very major one. They see that the people from Mexico, which are our brothers, come over on this side to work because the living conditions in Mexico are far worse than ours, they are poor. It is not their fault that they come and take our jobs, it is the fault of the U.S. Government which exploits our brother because they pay lower wages, and at the same time the Mexican Americans on this side are left without jobs, and they have to travel up North.[26]

In brief summary, the effect of the commuter system on the United States side of the border is felt primarily by the working poor who must compete with these commuters. Employment opportunities for American workers are reduced; wages are kept low; union organization is hampered; and seasonal migratory work becomes the prime alternative. Accordingly, the presence of the commuters seriously aggravates the already bleak economic situation caused by agricultural mechanization and population increase in the border region.

In defense of prevailing border employment practices Lamar B. Jones has written:

The commuter system is very much a tacit trade agreement because it permits Mexico to make direct export of unemployment and Mexico earns foreign exchanges through repatriation of commuter earnings. To further the analogy that commuters are merely part of a trade flow is the idea that commuters constitute indirect subsidy to United States businesses to offset foreign exporters' cost advantages in production of textiles and other products manufactured principally in Asia and Southern Europe.[27]

Accordingly Jones argues that the workers (mostly Chicanos) on the American side of the border should be eligible for special training and relocation allowances provided under the terms of the Trade Expansion Act of 1962. The relevant provisions of this act call for a determination by the Tariff Commission that American workers are suffering unemployment or underemployment due to increased imports granted under trade concession agreements.

Needless to say, the Tariff Commission has not to date made any such ruling. Moreover, it is a questionable procedure to view the commuter system itself in the same terms as a "trade agreement" between nations. Trade agreements are established to affect the shipment and production of tangible products and natural resources. In the United States, the Clayton Act of 1914 asserted "that the labor of a human being is not a commodity or article of commerce."[28] Laws that are designed to affect the transport of commodities should not be equated with the needs of human beings. What may be sound policy for the transport of electric components or men's undershirts may be quite inadequate when applied to the survival and prosperity of human life. To say that the commuter system is but a trade agreement is to denigrate the value of human life to the level of an inanimate object. The commuter system serves to depress and to prevent improvements in working conditions for Chicanos. It is a system that would be intolerable to any other class of citizens but is sanctioned in this instance because the victims are the powerless poor.

A host of proposals have been offered to lessen the effects of the commuter system. Among them are its immediate termination, regularization of the labor certification process to require periodic reviews rather than simply the initial determination of the impact of the green-carder, establishment of a nonresident work permit with regular review decisions, installation of a commuter tax on employers, issuance of a commuter ticket that would be purchased by those who cross the border for employment, and the launching of a local drive by border employers to give preference to U.S. residents. The U.S. Civil Rights Commission has also heard recommendations that sanctions be imposed against U.S. employers who knowingly employ white-carders and that specific limitations be placed upon the time a green-carder can stay before making it mandatory that he become a U.S. citizen. Another comprehensive study contends that current border employment practices violate Title VII of the Civil Rights Act of 1964.[29] The contention is based upon the ban on discrimination on the basis of national origin contained in the law. By favoring Mexican nationals, it is alleged that the law is being violated. The U.S. Department of Labor claims that the economic slump in the United States in the late 1960s-early 1971 period has reduced the significance of the green card issue. Denial of labor certification has sharply curtailed the number of *new* green cards being issued. For those people already possessing such cards, of course, there has been no effect since the certification process is presently a "one time only" review. Moreover, it is logical to assume that once the economy recovers, the restrictive practices regarding card issuance will be relaxed once more.

MIGRATORY LABOR

The commuter issue is part of the explanation for the disproportionate number of Chicanos who compose the migratory farm labor pool. A 1969 U.S. Senate report concluded "that migrant farmworkers and their families were a forgotten minority, the neediest and the least served of any in America."[30] In 1967, migrant farmworkers numbered 276,000 or about 9 percent of the nation's total agricultural work force during that year. Although the percentage is small when compared with the nationwide agricultural employment figures, their presence is highly significant in the Southwest and other selected geographic areas and at certain times of the year for specified crops. It is estimated that about 25 percent of all migrants are Chicanos and that about 40 percent of Chicanos employed in agriculture are migrant workers.[31]

Although some migrant workers were employed in forty-six states in 1968, they were concentrated in the Southwest. The main causative factor for their predominance in the Southwest is that many crops of the region are grown under irrigation conditions. As water is scarce in these localities, the areas are sparsely populated. Hence, local labor supplies are inadequate to meet seasonal employment demands. Nearly 70 percent of total migrant employment in 1968 (in official jargon called "man-months of migratory worker employment") occurred in nine states: California, Florida, Michigan, Texas, Washington, New Jersey, New York, Ohio, and Oregon. Of these nine states, California and Texas accounted for 31 percent of the combined total amount of employment. Unquestionably, most of the migrants in the Southwest are Chicanos. In 1968, for instance, south Texas pumped 88,700 farmworkers into the migratory stream, not counting thousands more family members who accompanied these migrants.

The deprived economic status of migratory workers is too well known to be recounted. No one becomes a migrant farmworker if he has any possible alternative way of making a living. The work is physically demanding, it is poorly paid, and accordingly it attracts only those who have no options. Yet these people by their daily endeavors demonstrate an amazing adherence to the Protestant work ethic. The noted psychiatrist Robert Coles has concluded from his famous study of "the migrant subculture" that

. . . [the] issue is social and economic, not psychological: the American farmhands I have studied and observed are motivated toward work, want to work, and will work. Other workers may well

43

be preferred by farmowners, but psychiatric observations do not support many of the claims frequently made about the laziness of farmhands. On the contrary, most of these people display an initiative and desire for work in striking contrast to their poor brethren in cities, many of whom are unemployed and on relief, some of whom are unable to work, and some eventually uninterested in looking for any possibility of work. Migrant farmworkers, almost by definition, show a remarkable capacity and desire to travel far and wide in search of work.[32]

The fact that in 1968 about 100,000 of the nation's migratory workers came from the southwestern border region of the nation means that understanding and remedial attention should be directed here. Large numbers of green and white card commuters find employment in agriculture in these very border regions that spawn the single greatest source of migratory workers. Although an end of the commuter system would not stop the migratory exodus from the border areas, it would lessen the pressure. Another significant factor would be a vigorous crackdown on illegal entrants who flood into the farm labor force. A 1970 study of the border economy disclosed that 72 percent of the illegal entrants were employed in agriculture.[33] It is likely that farm employment provides the single greatest source of employment for these illegal entrants. While it is true that Mexico would likely raise objections to curtailing the commuter system, it could hardly object to more stringent controls placed upon the illegal entrants.

It follows that unless and until some measure of control of the quantitative supply of labor is adopted, the outlook of human resource development efforts in the rural economy of the Southwest is dim.

THE "TWIN PLANTS" PROGRAM

Following the termination of the bracero program in 1964, unemployment in northern Mexico began to soar from its already inordinately high levels. No longer was it legally possible for a substantial number of Mexican males to find seasonal employment as American farmworkers. Responding to the problem, the government of Mexico launched the Mexican Border Industries Program (known as Programa de Industrializacion Fronterizo) in 1965.

Under this program, the Mexican government created a free trade industrial zone which extends twelve miles in from the border along its entire length. Simultaneously in 1965, American tariff regulations were revised as a form of compensation to Mexico for the cessation of the bracero program. The "offshore operations" of American- or Mexican-owned assembly factories were to be assessed only a 10 percent tax on the value added to the products in Mexico. As most of the work is assembling electrical component parts and textile products, most of the value added consists simply of wages. With the prevailing minimum wage in Mexico varying from $2.24 to $3.68 *a day,* there is a considerable reduction in the assembly costs to the American enterprises. Mexico, in turn, does *not* apply any duties on these exports. Thus, unassembled goods are shipped from American plants to Mexico for final assembly before being brought back into the American market. For this reason, the program is often referred to as the "twin plants" program because of the tandem operations involved.

American participation in the program accelerated after the U.S. Tariff Commission gave the program its implicit blessing in 1970. At that time, the commission concluded that repeal of 1965 tax provision would cause more harm than good for the United States. The rationale was that "repeal would probably result in only a modest number of jobs returned to the U.S., which likely would be more than offset by the loss of jobs among workers now producing components for export and those who further process the imported products."[34]

By 1971, 333 plants, almost all of which were American

owned, were participating in the program. Among the firms are many of the nation's largest concerns—Bendix, Zenith, Lockheed, RCA, Honeywell, and Samsonite. They produced $350 million worth of goods under the terms of the program plus another $150 million worth of export items that were not subject to the special tariff arrangements. It was estimated in 1971 that 40,000 Mexicans were employed in these border ventures.

The "twin plants" has come to represent the height of contradictions. It was set up in response to unemployment problems of male farmworkers but the assembling work employs mostly females. Moreover, since 1960 when Mexico initiated its National Frontier Program (known as Programa Nacional Fronterizo, or PRONAF), the national goal was espoused to promote the location of Mexican industry in the border zone. The objective of PRONAF is to reduce Mexican dependence upon the United States by enabling Mexican produced goods to compete more effectively with American retail goods, but the Mexican Border Industries program has significantly increased the dependency of the Mexican border economy upon the actions of American business. It seems, then, that the endeavor is counter to Mexico's proclaimed development strategy as manifested by PRONAF.

Tragically there is scant mention of the difficulties raised by the program on the American side of the border. Although it has reduced some of the incentive for Mexicans to cross into the United States to find employment, the Border Industries program has also aggravated the ability to attract industry and to improve wages and working conditions on the American side. The possible advantage that the prevailing low wage structure along the American side of the border (relative to the rest of the nation) might afford in attracting American industry to its environs is nullified by the even lower wages available on the Mexican side. It is absolutely impossible to conceive of a similar situation being allowed to exist and to be officially sanctioned in any other area of the United States. The Chicanos, especially those being forced out of agriculture by mechanization, now must witness the purposeful sacrifice of numerous chances for economic development, industrial diversification, and employment opportunities in their home region. Again, the frequent alternative for many Chicanos is to move to an urban barrio [district] where they must compete for positions on the lowest rung of the urban economic ladder.

NOTES

1. George I. Sánchez, "History, Culture, and Education," in *La Raza: Forgotten Americans* (South Bend: University of Notre Dame, 1966), p. 9.

2. "Farm Workers," Staff Report Prepared by the U.S. Commission of Civil Rights, *Hearings* (Washington, D.C.: U.S. Government Printing Office, 1969), p. 953. Hereinafter referred to as *Hearings*.

3. A small number of Filipinos are employed as farm workers in California. With this exception, the "Spanish-speaking" as it applies to agricultural workers in the Southwest is virtually identical with Chicanos. There is little evidence of the presence of Cubans or Puerto Ricans. It is true that some Puerto Ricans are employed in agriculture, but they are predominantly in the Northeast and the Southeast and most work under special and supervised programs between the government of the United States and that of the Commonwealth of Puerto Rico.

4. "Statement of Representative John C. Box," *Congressional Record*, 71st Cong., 2nd sess. (February 9, 1928), vol. 69, part 3, pp. 2817–18.

5. Carey McWilliams, *North from Mexico* (New York: Greenwood Press, 1968), pp. 270–71.

6. Lamar B. Jones, "Mexican American Labor Problems in Texas" (unpublished Ph.D. dissertation, University of Texas at Austin, 1965), p. 5.

7. David S. North, *Alien Workers: A Study of the Labor Certification Program* (Washington, D.C.: Trans Century Corporation, August 1971), p. 69.

8. Michael Mallory, "Human Wave of Mexicans Splashes Across Border," *The National Observer,* October 16, 1971, p. 1.

9. David S. North, *The Border Crossers: People Who Live in Mexico and Work in the United States* (Washington, D.C.: Trans Century Corporation, 1970), p. 135.

10. Ibid., p. 72.

11. "The Commuter on the United States-Mexico Border," Staff report of the U.S. Commission on Civil Rights in *Hearings*, p. 983.

12. North, *Alien Workers*, pp. 95–96.

13. North, *The Border Crossers*, pp. 95–96.

14. Ibid., p. 205.

15. Ibid.

16. Ibid., pp. 209–10.

17. Anna-Stina Ericson, "The Impact of Commuters on the Mexican-American Border Area," *Monthly Labor Review* (August 1970) vol. 93, no. 8, p. 18 [emphasis is supplied].

18. U.S. Commission on Civil Rights, *Hearings*, p. 985.

19. Leo Grebler *et al., The Mexican American People* (New York: Free Press, 1970), p. 73.

20. U.S. Commission on Civil Rights, *Hearings*, p. 985.

21. Ibid., p. 987.

22. Fred H. Schmidt, *Spanish Surnamed Americans Employment in the Southwest* (Washington, D.C.: U.S. Government Printing Office, 1970), p. 62.

23. See Brian S. Rungeling, "Impact of Mexican Alien Commuters on the Apparel Industry of El Paso: A Case Study" (unpublished Ph.D. dissertation, University of Kentucky, 1969).

24. Ericson, "The Impact of Commuters," p. 20.

25. U.S. Commission on Civil Rights, *Hearings*, p. 998.

26. Ibid., p. 461. Mr. Ramirez is employed by VISTA in Laredo, Texas.

27. Lamar B. Jones, "Alien Commuters in United States Labor Markets," *International Migration Review* (Spring, 1970), p. 83.

28. Section 6, the Act of October 15, 1914, c. 323, 38 Stat. 730 (more popularly known as the Clayton Act).

29. Schmidt, *Spanish Surnamed Americans*, p. 46.

30. "The Migratory Farm Labor Problem in the United States," *1969 Report* of the Committee on Labor and Public Welfare of the U.S. Senate, 91st Cong., 1st sess. (February 19, 1969), p. 25.

31. Ibid., p. 5.

32. Ibid., pp 17–18.

33. North, *The Border Crossers,* p. 132.

34. "Spread of U.S. Plants to Mexico Brings a Boom—And Complaints," *U.S. News and World Report,* vol. 72, no. 13 (March 27, 1972), p. 59.

5

The Effect of General Agricultural Employment Policies

Regardless of his race or ethnic group, the legal status of anyone employed in the agricultural sector of the American economy is that of a second-class citizen. Although large farm owners are the most privileged group in American corporate society (with import quota protection, antitrust law exemptions, price supports, soil bank purchases, subsidized research, irrigation, land reclamation, and erosion projects, and special property tax rates), farmworkers survive only by the law of the jungle. In no sector of the economy does Michael Harrington's famous thesis that the welfare state has brought the benefits of socialism to the rich and the horrors of laissez-faire to the poor seem to be more vividly exemplified.

Agricultural workers across the nation have been either excluded or given reduced coverage from the basic social legislation that nonagricultural workers have come to take for granted. Among these are minimum wage protection, unemployment insurance, workman's compensation, and the guaranteed right to bargain collectively. The absence of these basic assurances has significant manpower implications. The quantity and the quality of the workers in the industry are no doubt influenced by the prevailing employment and working conditions.

With the inordinately high concentration of Chicanos who are dependent upon agriculture for their livelihood, developments in the industry are a major determinate of Chicano well-being. The status of farmworker coverage by social legislation in the five Southwestern states is presented in table 5.

MINIMUM WAGE COVERAGE

As indicated in an earlier chapter, the gap in relative wages between agricultural and nonagricultural workers has continually widened since the end of World War II. In the Southwest, no state minimum wage, where applicable, would bring the worker up *to* the minimum poverty income level even if it were possible to secure year-round employment. There are numerous exemptions from the requirement to pay even these paltry wages. In Texas, for example, all family members of a covered breadwinner are exempted if the family resides on the premises of the employer. All states exclude from coverage "hand harvest laborers" who "customarily and generally" have been paid on a piece rate basis.

As for the federal minimum wage coverage, it was not until 1966 that farmworkers were extended limited coverage under the Fair Labor Standards Act. Beginning at $1.00 an hour in 1967, it increased gradually to $1.30 an hour as of February 1, 1969, for covered workers. To be covered, workers must be employed by employers using more than 500 mandays of farm labor in any calendar quarter of the preceding calendar year. As a result, the wage in 1969 applied to less than 1 percent of all farms and less than 400,000 of over 3 million farmworkers. All farmworkers are excluded from the overtime pay provisions of the act. Because of lack of knowledge of its existence and because enforcement authority is scant, it is acknowledged that the act has had questionable impact even for the limited numbers it theoretically embraces.

Table 5. Status of state laws in the Southwest pertaining to farmworkers as of December 1, 1967 (unless otherwise noted)

State	Compensation	Minimum wage	Overtime wage coverage	Unemployment and Workmen's Compensation	Housing
California	Compulsory	$1.65 for women and $1.35 for minors (16 to 18 yrs.)	Exempt	Disability insurance is provided for most workers	Mandatory standards
New Mexico	Voluntary, at discretion of employer	$1.30 (as of 1969)	Exempt	None	Mandatory standards
Texas	None	$1.10 (as of 1970)	Exempt	None	None
Colorado	Voluntary, at discretion of employer	None	None	None	Mandatory standards
Arizona	Compulsory	None	None	None	Mandatory standards

SOURCE: "Farm Workers," *Hearings*, Staff Report of the U.S. Commission on Civil Rights (Washington, D.C.: U.S. Government Printing Office, 1969), p. 957. The above table includes author's updated material.

There is limited evidence, however, that the effect of the $1.00 minimum that was first applied in 1967 did cause wages to rise without noticeably accelerating the decline in agricultural employment.[1] There were, of course, other factors at work—increasing mechanization and farm consolidation into large producing units—which may have contributed to increased productivity, which would allow money wage advances with minimal employment effects.

There are other reasons to believe that neither the extension of coverage nor the raising of the benefit levels has to date had a detrimental effect upon the level of agricultural employment in the Southwest. An across-the-board increase in cost that affects a major portion of the volume producing units of the industry should have an inconsequential effect on the demand for agricultural products. These products tend to be demand inelastic—changes in the price of products tend to have little influence upon the quantity demanded. Moreover, it is conceivable that an increase in wages can lead to greater productivity by attracting better qualified workers and by inducing more efficient management practices. If so, productivity increases can offset cost increases so as to leave employment unaffected.

There is no evidence that the existing minimum wage laws in agriculture have had any adverse effects for the farm employer. Certainly, farm workers deserve to receive the same benefit levels and overtime coverage as nonfarm workers. The time to extend legislative equality to farm workers is long overdue.

Aside from the general issue of application of the federal minimum wage to agriculture, there is a special case of federally imposed wage determination which needs to be mentioned. Namely, it is the Sugar Act of 1937 which has application to some Chicanos who are migratory workers. Under this act, federal subsidies were made available to domestic producers of beet sugar and cane sugar. To qualify for the subsidy, however, it is necessary that the grower pay a wage no lower than that annually set by the U.S. Department of Agriculture. The wage rates are set geographically and by crop (i.e., sugar beets or sugar cane). They are set by an open hearing. In practice, there is seldom any spokesman available for the workers, who are usually unorganized by any union. The growers and refiners, however, have organized expertise available through their associations. When the workers have had spokesmen, they have not been competent to meet the arguments of the producers. Accordingly, in his pioneering study of the farm labor market in the United States, Lloyd Fisher has reported:

The result has been in a sense worse than if the gesture had not been made. The wage thus established has tended strongly to become the wage paid. Though declared as a minimum wage, it has commonly been the only wage, supported by the sanction of government action and presented often by the growers to the workers as a wage which had become mandatory by government decree.[2]

For the Southwest, the applicable wage is that set for sugar beets in California and Colorado. Effective April 1969, the minimum wage was $1.65 an hour with exceptions for various hand labor operations in which fixed wages per acre prevailed. Deductions are permitted for meals and transportation costs provided by employers.

UNEMPLOYMENT INSURANCE COVERAGE

With the exception of the District of Columbia (whose program is federalized), unemployment insurance coverage is determined by the respective states of the union. As indicated in table 5, no southwestern state has elected to extend unemployment insurance to farmworkers. Countless efforts have been made to provide such coverage but to date they have been

53

to no avail. In 1970 an attempt was made at the federal level (as a part of the Employment Security Amendments of 1970) to extend uniform coverage to all farms with 300 man-days of hired farm labor within any calendar quarter. The effort failed to survive a congressional conference committee. Had it passed, it is estimated that its provisions would have applied nationally to 572,000 farmworkers employed on 67,000 farm enterprises.

Resistance to the inclusion of farmworkers in the Southwest in unemployment insurance systems stems from political and not economic considerations. Farmworkers in Hawaii are covered by such a program as are sugar cane workers in Puerto Rico. From the experience of these two groups, there is no reason to believe that there are any unique problems that should preclude extension of coverage uniformly to all farmworkers. Indeed, a careful study by the U.S. Department of Labor in 1971 of the topic concluded that

the findings in these research efforts, in combination with the known changes taking place in agriculture, make continued exclusion of agricultural employment anachronistic. . . . All available evidence indicates that no insurmountable obstacles would arise in providing this needed and long overdue protection to a farmworker to whom the consequences of involuntary unemployment are at least equal to those of his societal brothers now covered under this program.[3]

Here again is a public policy gap whose time to be filled has come.

WORKMEN'S COMPENSATION COVERAGE

Despite the fact that agriculture is the nation's third most hazardous industry (its fatality and injury rates are exceeded only by mining and construction), mandatory workmen's compensation protection is seldom available. In the Southwest, only California has extended coverage to farmworkers on the same basis as all other workers. The absence of such programs means that injured farmworkers are denied income during a time of disability, rehabilitation training opportunities, and access to medical services. In the case of a fatal accident on the job, this exclusion from workmen's compensation protection means the family of the deceased is not eligible for death and burial benefits.

Originally, the rationale for excluding agricultural workers was that the industry was not mechanized and therefore not very hazardous. Such is hardly the case today. Moreover, the increasing use of herbicides and pesticides with their yet unknown effects on farmworkers makes this lack of protection even more inhumane.

A related development of possible long range significance has been the extension of the Occupational Safety Act of 1970 to agricultural workers. It is a rare instance in which farmworkers have been given equal federal protection with non-farm workers. The act calls for federal government enforcement of industrial safety standards. The Occupational Safety and Health Appeals Commission was established to administer the act. Employers are required to provide work sites that are free of hazards to workers. The secretary of labor is empowered to set forth the prevailing standards. The secretary may approve the state standards if they exist and if they are at least the equivalent of those issued by the federal government. The act also calls for a comprehensive study of the effectiveness and adequacy of existing state workmen's compensation laws. The void of coverage of most farmworkers should be high on the agenda of any reform proposals from such a study.

There can be no justification for the absence of available and adequate workmen's compensation for all farmworkers. The accumulated experience of the 6 states which provide protection on an equal basis with all other workers (as well as the other 14 states which provide some form of coverage to some agricultural workers) has shown that equal coverage for farmworkers is a viable program as well as the humane thing to do. If all states do not move to provide such coverage, the federal government should create a system of coverage. The precedents for such action do exist. Since passage of the Longshoremen's and Harbor Worker's Compensation Act in 1927, privately employed workers in longshoring and related maritime employment have had a separate workmen's compensation program with direct federal administration by the Department of Labor. Moreover, this legislation has been significantly broadened to encompass a vast array of sundry industries and workers by successive amendments to include all forms of private employment in the District of Columbia (1928); to include any employee at a military defense facility both at home and abroad (1942); to include any employee of a private contractor who does work for the government in a war zone (1942); to include any employee of a private company involved in off-shore exploration for natural resources (1952); and to include any employee of unappropriated fund instrumentalities of the armed forces such as post exchanges and motion picture services (1958). The point is that there is ample room for farmworkers under this broad act if the federal government sincerely believes that the time has come to end the tragic era of agricultural exclusion from such a basic form of social insurance. Ideally, the act could serve as a precedent for the establishment of an entirely separate program for farmworkers at the federal level.

THE PROTECTED RIGHT TO BARGAIN COLLECTIVELY

Farmworkers are not covered by the National Labor Relations Act (NLRA). Accordingly, there is no stipulation that requires recognition of a bargaining unit or good faith bargaining over wages, hours, and working conditions, or regulation of unfair labor practices. In 1968, an effort was made to extend coverage of the law to farms with twelve or more employees and an annual wage bill of at least $10,000 a year. It was estimated that only about 1.4 percent of the total farms in the nation would be affected and that about 622,000 farmworkers would be included. With the large farms and ranches that dominate the Southwest, the effect could have been significant for many Chicanos. The bill failed due to both overwhelming opposition and underwhelming support.

Cesar Chavez, the director of the United Farm Workers Organizing Committee (UFWOC), has expressed second thoughts concerning the desirability of blanket coverage of agricultural workers under the existing National Labor Relations Act as amended. Chavez believes that agricultural unionism needs the same period of prolabor legislation that the Wagner Act of 1935 afforded other industrial unions before the basic act was made restrictive to labor by the amendments and additions of the Taft-Hartley Act (1947) and the Landrum-Griffin Act (1959). As he puts it, "we too need our decent period of time to grow strong under the life-giving sun of a public policy which affirmatively favors the growth of farm unionism."[4] Thus, Chavez seeks NLRA coverage subject to the following three modifying conditions:

1. Exemption for a time from the Taft-Hartley provisions which restrict traditional union activity, especially the ban on recognition picketing and the so-called secondary boycott, made especially repressive by the mandatory injunction in both cases.
2. Exemption from the operation of Taft-Hartley Section 14(b) which makes misnamed state "right to work" laws operative in interstate commerce.
3. It should be made an unfair labor practice for a grower to employ anyone during a strike or lockout who has not actually a permanent residence in the United States.[5]

With respect to state labor relations acts, fourteen states had such statutes as of 1969. The only southwestern state with such legislation is Colorado, and its law does not cover agricultural workers.

The use of collective bargaining in agriculture has traditionally incurred strong grower opposition. The principle contention has been that agriculture is distinct from nonagricultural activity due to the vulnerability of employers to strikes at harvest time. In response, supporters of collective bargaining contend that the possible damage encountered by an employer in nonagricultural industries has never been considered a sufficient justification to deny statutory coverage. Furthermore, there is also the implied belief that a harvest time strike—if it actually materialized—would be successful. This is dubious since it is counter to the best interests of a union to bankrupt their employer. It is conceivable that a contractual pledge could be secured by employers from the union which would agree not to strike at harvest time in exchange for other more desirable concessions (e.g., a hiring hall system of job referral). Above all, there is no reason to believe that collective bargaining is incompatible with agricultural conditions. As one study of rural labor markets concluded ". . . that it was *political expediency and the powerlessness of farmworkers* that led to their exclusion from coverage [under the NLRA] rather than any administrative or economic differences between agricultural and non-agricultural workers." [6]

There are, of course, other obstacles to agricultural unionism than merely the lack of National Labor Relations Act (or a state equivalent) protections. One is the fact that workers are scattered over a vast geographical area. Accordingly, organizational costs are high and farmworkers' incomes are low. Moreover, in the Southwest especially, there is an abundance of potential strikebreakers in the form of illegal entrants, green-carders, and other underemployed indigenous rural nonfarm workers and technologically displaced former farm-workers. The presence of large numbers of migratory workers for whom the appeal of a permanent union is likely to be minimal only adds to organizational difficulties.

By the same token, there are forces at work that may ultimately enhance the prospects of a successful union movement in agriculture. Most notable of these is the consolidation of agricultural production into fewer but larger units. Also, as the national grape boycott of the mid-sixties demonstrates, there is some element of public sympathy for efforts to improve the deplorable conditions under which farmworkers work and live.

The fact that NLRA coverage is presently unavailable to agricultural workers does not, of course, mean that collective bargaining is prohibited. It simply means that there are no legal protections available to those who seek to be union members and to bargain collectively. The worker may join a union but an employer is free to fire him for such an action. Furthermore, the lack of NLRA coverage means that there is no way to conduct representation elections or to certify an exclusive bargaining agent or to regulate unfair labor practices by either employers or unions.

Collective bargaining, as a system of dispute settlement, is based upon the relative power of the participants as well as the ability to inflict and withstand economic losses. If agricultural unions can secure sufficient power, they can gain recognition with or without legislative assistance. To date, however, it has been very difficult to marshall the needed power for a successful organizational campaign. To overcome this deficiency, Cesar Chavez has made an effort to broaden his unionizing effort to encompass community organization and to enlist nationwide consumer boycotts. Legislative protections will not automatically secure or guarantee maintenance of collective bargaining for farmworkers. They will, however, establish a system for the resolution of recognitional conflicts and the prevention of unfair labor practices. Clearly, such a development is a step in the right direction for both farmworkers and the nation as a whole.

ADDITIONAL POLICY AREAS

There have been several special enactments that have affected rural Chicanos that were passed during the 1960s. Among these are the Bilingual Education Act (passed as Title VII of the Elementary and Secondary School Act Amendments in 1967) and amendments to Title I of the same act which provided compensatory education funds to migratory workers for the first time. The earlier Migrant Children Educational Assistance Act of 1960 and the Migrant Health Act of 1962 represented the initial breakthroughs of federal legislation pertaining to the welfare of migratory workers. These programs, however, were based upon matching funds being made available to state initiated projects. In addition, the Farm Labor Contractor Registration Act of 1963 was enacted in response to abuses by unscrupulous crewleaders. Also, the Interstate Commerce Commission has instituted regulations affecting the transportation of three or more farmworkers for a distance of 75 miles or more across state boundaries. The regulations pertain to equipment safety, required rest stops, seats for passengers, and regular driver changes. With regard to the intrastate transportation of farmworkers, only one southwestern state, California, has provided similar state regulations.

Even though most Chicano migratory workers are poor, they are seldom eligible for welfare assistance. Most states have residency requirements which mean migrant workers and their families are usually denied eligibility for welfare assistance and food stamps. Moreover, in many rural areas, administrative discrimination and limited local funds preclude the rural poor from receiving welfare benefits.

As for child labor, the Fair Labor Standards Act (FLSA) of 1938 does forbid the employment of any person under the age of sixteen years during school hours. The FLSA prohibits the employment of a child under fourteen years at any time. Yet, the prevailing pattern for Chicanos, especially migrant workers, is to work together as a family in the fields, and laws never enforce themselves.

NOTES

1. Anna F. Carrera, "The Effects of the Federal Minimum Wage on Hired Farmworkers," *Farm Labor Developments* (May 1968), pp. 12–20.

2. Lloyd Fisher, *The Harvest Labor Market in California* (Cambridge: Harvard University Press, 1953), p. 107.

3. "The Farmworker and Unemployment Insurance," *Rural Manpower Developments* (September-October 1971), p. 21.

4. "Statement of Cesar E. Chavez, Director, United Farm Workers Organizing Committee, AFL-CIO," *Hearings on Agricultural Labor Legislation* before the Subcommittee on Labor of the Committee on Labor and Public Welfare of the U.S. Senate, 91st Cong., 1st sess. (Washington, D.C.: U.S. Government Printing Office, 1969), p. 23.

5. Ibid.

6. Ray Marshall, *Policy and Program Issues in Rural Manpower Development* (mimeographed material; Austin: Center for the Study of Human Resources, 1971), p. 54.

61

6

The Influence of Manpower Policy

The impact of the "manpower revolution" of the 1960s upon the rural labor market for Chicanos has been so soft as to leave little imprint. The nationwide thrust of manpower policy has been upon the improvement of the employment potential of urban workers. Yet although *all* rural workers have been neglected relative to urban workers, there is ample reason to believe that Chicano rural workers have been ignored even more than either rural Anglos or rural blacks.

GENERAL OBSTACLES

There are several reasons why, in general, rural workers tend to be ignored. First, there is the problem of politics. Training slots for institutional MDTA (Manpower Development and Training Act) classes, MDTA on-the-job training, Neighborhood Youth Corps, New Careers, Special Impact, and Work Incentive programs represent dollars, and dollars represent patronage. When push comes to shove, urban areas have had more muscle in securing these undertakings. The competition for supporting funds usually combines the vested interests of public schools, vocational schools, community action agencies, and junior colleges with the lobbying strength of city governments, organized community pressure groups, unions, and corporate interests. As one Texas official of the Rural Manpower Services of the U.S. Department of Labor put it: "when the state politicos divvy up the manpower money, the rural areas don't get nothing."[1]

Second, the adults in many rural areas fear that the formal training afforded under these programs is designed to prepare young people for jobs that can be had only by migrating to a city. The result, of course, is that despite opposition from their elders the young people leave, and in the city suffer severely from inadequate academic preparation and the absence of exposure to vocational education classes in anything other than agriculturally related subjects.

A third factor is that the downtrodden who live in rural areas have a severe "audibility gap." In urban areas, civil disorder and collective action have served as a prod to manpower program enactments. In rural areas, the population is diffused, and the opportunities to threaten, picket, sit in, or burn down are sparse. Who knows or is really concerned with how many grass fires have been started, fences cut, stones thrown, curses shouted, or fists shaken by anguished rural souls? In a city, such conduct seldom goes unnoticed or unpublicized.

SPECIFIC OBSTACLES

With specific regard to Chicanos in rural poverty, there is an additional factor. Since they are concentrated in the Southwest, the Chicanos are virtually unknown to most Americans. Because of this, they have been neglected in the formulation of program designs and in the staffing of program operations. The civil rights movement of the 1960s did not result in immediate public concern for the plight of Chicanos. It seems that the impetus given by this social movement to the development of manpower policies has had the needs of Chicanos only as an afterthought.

With respect to the ability to initiate national awareness of Chicano problems, it is ironic that the Chicano leaders with national reputations are singularly associated with rural life. The "la causa" movement of Cesar Chavez is centered upon organizational needs of farm workers in central California; the "la alianza" movement of Reis Lopez Tijerina focuses upon land claims of rural families in northern New Mexico; and the "la raza" movement of José Angel Gutierrez has had its most noteworthy successes in securing educational and community reforms in rural cities of south Texas (especially in the small rural outpost of Crystal City, but also in Del Rio, Kingsville, Uvalde, Edcouch, and Elsa, all of which are strongly tied to the agricultural economy of the region). Sad to say, these movements have captured most of the national attention that has been paid to Chicano well-being and have fostered the mistaken impression that most of their needs are nonurban.

A disproportionate amount of manpower programs and services for Chicanos has been assistance to migratory workers. Even in their case, however, the remedies have focused upon health, transportation, housing, and personal treatment. Little attention has been given to occupational training. Such a pattern, as will be discussed shortly, is the general characteristic of all existing manpower policy throughout the rural Southwest.

PROGRAMS FOR MIGRATORY WORKERS

The Chicano migratory workers are among the most disadvantaged of all residents of the Southwest. Migrants suffer many disabilities that are associated with their mobility and the conditions under which they live and work. However, the dimensions of the migrant problem *per se* are being reduced by mechanization, which has sharply reduced migrant employment. To date, many measures have been adopted to deal with the problems of migrants, but most have had limited effectiveness because they did not get at the root of the problem. Precisely speaking, the fact is that migrant workers are forced—by competition from illegal Mexican entrants and commuters for the scarce jobs available in their home base—to travel to find employment opportunities. Until existing programs incorporate an awareness of this feature, projects designed to entice migrants out of the migrant stream are unlikely to be effective. A successful program to improve the plight of migrant workers must be comprehensive in scope. It must include methods of reducing the unfair competition for jobs in their home base. In addition, it is necessary to improve wages and benefits of those who work in agriculture so as to enhance the attractiveness of the jobs to nonfarm workers in local rural labor markets and reduce the migrancy demand.

The existing difficulty in providing manpower services to migrant workers is their mobility. Most manpower programs—as well as the standard social, welfare, educational, and political institutions of society—are designed to serve stable constituencies. Nevertheless, piecemeal programs have sought to reach and to serve migrant workers where they can seasonally be found.

There have been attempts to reach a solution to the seasonal workers' problem. In 1954 the Annual Worker Plan (AWP) began. Seeking to reduce the time between jobs, AWP tried to coordinate the demand and the supply for migrants. The public employment services in the supply states were to ascertain the available number of migrants while the employment services in the demand states were to determine the number of needed workers. From this information, schedules were prepared for the various crew leaders. Use of AWP has declined sharply since 1967 partly because of the inroads of mechanization but, more importantly, because of the increasing refusal of growers to participate. It seems that during this era, new housing standards were required by the Federal government, effective July 1, 1967 (as well as more stringent standards by some of the states where migrants worked). Rather than comply with the standards and continue to participate in AWP, many growers have sought to leapfrog the program and to contract directly with crew leaders with whom they have dealt for years.

In 1969 the Department of Labor initiated a migrant demonstration project in Texas which was designed to assist migrants who wished to leave the migrant stream to do so, and to provide a battery of social services for those who wished to remain migrants. Local employment service offices were to employ rural outreach interviewers (ROI's) whose task was to work specifically with migrants. The objective was to change the image and, in fact, the practices of the local employment services away from being exclusively a hiring agent of employers toward a role that is responsive to the needs of workers.[2] Associated with this 10-state undertaking was a special experimental and demonstration project in Texas that was to involve 784 families (with a total of 6,250 members). The migrant demonstration project failed to accomplish its mission. For lack of an adequate evaluation, it is impossible to find the precise causes. The main reason cited for the program's failure was its inability to reach migrants who were actually in the migrant stream. It seems that the most difficult problem confronting program officials was the process of determining who was a migrant. A knowledgeable official of the Rural Manpower Service stated, "it is not easy for a migrant to get into the migrant program."[3] Some of the criteria used for admission were to hold American citizenship; be a male; have a minimum of an eighth-grade education; and have earned at least 50 percent of the previous year's income from agricultural employment. The education requirement seems especially arbitrary for a migratory worker program. It is small wonder the program had to turn to "nonmigrants" to find a clientele. Another factor, it seems, was the inability of Texas officials to secure the cooperation of employment service officials in other grower states (demand states) who were not interested in rendering services to "Texas Mexicans." These states, it seems, found migrants desirable as workers but "untouchables" if the prospect was that they might settle permanently in their communities.

Nonetheless, the ROI's did assist some migrants to find housing, to obtain improved health care, and to locate jobs. Also the ROI's accomplished a great deal in making manpower, welfare, and education agencies more responsive to the migrant's needs. After two years, however, the special program was discontinued, and the public employment services in the respective states were supposed to build services for migrants into their regular procedures.

In 1971 the Department of Labor announced a new program—"the last yellow bus" (an overt symbol of the method for transporting migratory workers)—which was designed to assist in the transition of migrant workers from farm to nonfarm employment. The program grew out of the aforementioned migrant experiment and demonstration project and was designed to settle out 5,800 migrants the first year. The strategy is to provide both training and job development in the home base area and programs to settle people out of the migrant stream. Mobility facilitation units seek to coordinate services from central locations along the migratory stream. Manpower specialists attached to these units will be able to provide job development, basic education, occupational counseling, supplementary training, and financial assistance. Instead of restricting recruitment only to Texas, as did the earlier migrant program, "the last yellow bus" will seek out participants anywhere they can be found in the migrant stream.

The fact that the demand for migrants is receding sharply should mean that many of these workers will be vitally in need of alternatives. Recruitment should not be a problem. In addition, as numerous studies have found, migrant workers are such not because of any particular love for the vocation but rather because it is a necessity for which they have scant alternatives. "Yellow bus" hopes to provide choices. Yet, although migrants are certainly a most disadvantaged group, they have received more attention than the more numerous but needy rural nonmigrants whose economic state is at least as bad if not worse.[4]

THE RURAL MANPOWER SERVICE

As an outgrowth of the efforts which began in the early 1960s to establish a "comprehensive manpower policy" for the nation, the rural sector of the economy has been incorporated into the planning and programs of the era. Relative to the universe of recognized need of disadvantaged Americans, however, the apportionment of manpower funds and the level of program activity between urban and rural sectors has never approached being proportionate. Rural manpower services represent the weak sister whose cries for assistance are answered only as afterthoughts. Consequently, rural citizens have suffered from their low priority status. In the Southwest, as indicated earlier, Chicanos are the least urbanized of the major racial and ethnic groups of the region. They have had the most to lose from the paucity of attention.

In 1969 the Farm Labor Service, whose reputation in the Southwest was synonomous with servitude to employer needs, was reorganized by the U.S. Department of Labor into the Farm Labor and Rural Manpower Service. Then in 1970, the title was changed again to the Rural Manpower Service (RMS). The objective of the reorganization was to change both its image and its actual role. More concern is to be given to the needs of rural workers and to the broad array of rural jobs that are nonagricultural in nature and which in fact dominate the rural economy.

Since the effectiveness of the RMS in its new role is yet to be experienced, the theoretical role is that of becoming an advocate of the rural sector in the design of manpower plans and the administration of manpower programs for the Department of Labor. On paper the long run mission of RMS is laudable. The provision of rural manpower services to date has suffered immeasurably by a shortage of available manpower specialists who can write proposals, operate programs, and effectively state to the public the case for rural Americans.

Whether RMS can shift its focus away from the need to harvest crops toward that of serving people is an open question. In the spring of 1972, a report of a study conducted within the Department of Labor (which was brought about by an administrative complaint filed by 16 civil rights and farm worker organizations) accused RMS of pervasive discrimination against blacks and Chicanos. The report urged that the agency be staffed with rural workers to assure that the designated purpose to serve worker needs becomes a reality. The report called for more minority and bilingual staff members. It detailed instances in which established rules were not enforced—for instance, in Texas, job orders from employers frequently failed to state what wage was to be paid. In addition, it claimed that when minority workers sought assistance from RMS they were only "referred to the office handling agricultural employment without receiving any of the benefits of that office, such as testing, counseling, training, or being given consideration for non-agricultural placement services."[5] The review team added that minority workers, regardless of skills or previous work experience, were offered only agricultural jobs.

The usefulness of RMS to date has been largely conceptual. The need for a responsive rural manpower agency is real; the deed is yet to be performed.

NON-MIGRANT MANPOWER PROGRAMS

Although various manpower programs are operational in the rural Southwest, they are few in number, unclear in mission, small in size, and geographically scattered. In general, most rural residents are not even aware of the existence of many of them.[6] In urban areas, the Concentrated Employment Program (CEP) is the major delivery system for the Department of Labor's panoply of programs. In the rural Southwest, there are three CEP's. There is scant data available from these programs to draw strong exclusions. Since their inception in 1966, it is doubtful that more than 3,000 people (and these figures involve substantial double counting) have been served. The rural CEP's have developed a reputation for considerable flexibility given the severe restraints under which they operate. Yet the RMS has been critical of the CEP concept, in general, as applied to the rural situation. According to RMS, "the difficulty in adopting the concentrated aspect of the urban program model has been great; rural CEP's are very expensive and it is doubtful that the results justify the expense involved."[7]

A perennial problem of manpower programs in the rural Southwest has been the low wage structure and the inability to place program graduates into jobs for which they have been trained. This has been especially true for women in these programs. Frequently program enrollees receive higher incomes from the training allowances than they can earn upon leaving the program in the local economy. As a result, income maintenance, rather than skill endowment, has become the principle raison d'etre for many programs.

It is to the credit of the Department of Labor that its MDTA programs (as well as the manpower programs originally conceived under the Economic Opportunity Act—such as Job Corps, Neighborhood Youth Corps, etc.) insist that all participants be permanent residents of the United States and that they actually reside in the United States. The subterfuge that is tolerated by the Immigration and Naturalization Service—such as a postal mailbox address—is not allowed. Thus, program eligibility along the border areas and in the relevant rural areas is markedly reduced. Yet once the participant in one of these manpower programs completes his training, he must compete for the same scarce entry-level jobs that the green-carders, white-carders, illegal entrants, and non-trainees are also seeking.

With a surplus labor situation as a backdrop, it is logical that job creation programs rather than job training programs would dominate the program mix in the region. Operation Mainstream, a program that was created in 1965 as an amendment to the Economic Opportunity Act of 1964, has been widely used in rural areas where Chicanos are numerous. This program is designed to provide employment for adults of rural areas in beautification and conservation projects. As such, it does not challenge local power structures and therefore has proven to be very popular.[8] Operation Mainstream provides very little training or opportunities for job upgrading and it has done very little placement into private industry. It is a form of public service employment for adults. For youth, the Neighborhood Youth Corps, where it has been available, has served the identical purposes: to provide income and work experience in the public sector, but very little in the way of training.

In late 1971, the public service employment concept received an additional boost of support with the implementation of the Emergency Employment Act (EEA). Under EEA, federal funds are made available to state, county, and municipal units of government for employment of people to meet unmet public needs. The intent of the act is that these jobs be net additions to existing levels of employment and that the participants be moved into permanent slots as openings occur through normal attrition and growth. The allocation of funds was based upon a two-pronged formula relating both the absolute number of unemployed and the relative severity of unemployment. Under such a formula, all rural areas were discriminated against. Rural areas have notorious underemployment problems as well as discouraged workers which cause the number of people who are "officially" unemployed to be much lower than is actually the case.[9] Moreover, the formula for distribution for the first year was based upon the average employment in April, May, and June of 1971. In the Southwest, these are the months that the migratory workers are on the road and are fully employed. Had winter months been used or even an annual rate, the rural sectors of the states would have been entitled to more funds. As most of the states replicated the federal allocation formula in the distribution within their states, the distribution inadequacies were compounded against the rural populace.

The most difficult problems that rural areas in the Southwest have had with the EEA, however, have come more with the administrative guidelines of the act as promulgated by the Department of Labor. EEA, as is true of so many categorical programs, is written largely to meet the needs of urban populations. Rural needs are often assumed to be similar to urban needs despite mountains of evidence and experience to the contrary. Thus, guidelines, rules, regulations, and special issuances—for example, no EEA participant may be employed in an occupation in which any other non-EEA person is receiving a wage below the Federal minimum wages ($1.60 an hour)—are no problem in an urban setting. In the rural Southwest, they are an issue.[10] Similarly, the EEA administrative restrictions that severely restrict reimbursement of indirect costs or that require job descriptions and established personnel systems are no problem in big cities but seriously hamper (and, in some instances, prevent) rural participation. Thus, as one program official in Texas observed, "the Act does not fit the rural situation."[11] EEA, as administered in its first year, is antirural.

There is a desperate need for public service employment in the rural Southwest. But EEA or any similar venture must be given the latitude to serve the rural sector as it actually is and not be a carbon copy of the design for urban operations, which it is not.

NOTES

1. Personal interview with official of the regional office of the Rural Manpower Service, U.S. Department of Labor, Dallas, Texas, February 5, 1971.

2. Patricia Marshall, "From Migrant Stream to Mainstream," *Manpower,* vol. 3, no. 7 (July 1971), pp. 11-17.

3. Personal interview, February 5, 1971.

4. Ray Marshall, *Policy and Program Issues in Rural Manpower Development* (mimeographed material; Austin: Center for Study of Human Resources, 1971), p. 19.

5. "Rural Manpower Service Accused of Discrimination," *Austin American Statesman* (April 23, 1972), p. 1.

6. Ray Marshall, *Policy and Program Issues,* pp. 35–41.

7. Staff paper quoted in Ray Marshall, ibid., p. 34.

8. See Kirschner Associates, *National Evaluation of Operation Mainstream, Phase I: The Green Thumb-Green Light Program* (Albuquerque, N.M., January 1971) and *National Evaluation of Operation Mainstream, Phase II: The Senior Aides Program* (Albuquerque, N.M., May 1971).

9. Vernon M. Briggs, Jr., "The Emergency Employment Act of 1971: The Texas Experience," *The Emergency Employment Act: An Interim Assessment* (Washington, D.C.: U.S. Senate Committee on Labor and Public Welfare, 1972), pp. 153–86.

10. Ibid., pp. 172–74.

11. Vernon M. Briggs, Jr., "Texas," *The Emergency Employment Act: Second Interim Assessment* (Washington, D.C.: The National Manpower Policy Task Force, 1972), pp. 8–22.

7

Concluding Observations

Chicanos are disproportionately represented in both the migratory stream and the overall agricultural sector of the economy. The welfare of Chicanos who reside permanently in either rural America or urban areas but who work seasonally in rural occupations is intertwined with existing public policy measures. The economic plight of rural Chicanos is a classic example of administered social oppression. By purposefully denying the coverage by social legislation to workers on farms and in most small rural businesses and by allowing a continual flow of unskilled commuters and illegal entrants to depress prevailing working standards, Chicanos are often the victims of institutionally imposed and sanctioned poverty.

In an era in which many of "the new solutions" have become "the new problems," rural life still has all of the "old problems" to overcome. Before one can seriously consider initiating new proposals to develop job opportunities by attracting industry to rural areas or to expedite the migration of rural workers to urban areas, the current rules that govern rural working conditions should be rewritten. For Chicanos, the rural population is composed of two distinct groups: (1) single males, a group with a large number of green-carders and illegal entrants among their ranks, and (2) inordinately large families, who are the permanent rural population and the migratory families. Both groups suffer severe age, educational, training, language, and health handicaps relative to their urban Chicano counterparts. Nothing could be gained by encouraging these people to seek urban employment.

There is no monistic solution to the disadvantagement of the Chicano rural labor force and their families. An obvious beginning is to regulate the flow of entrants into the rural economy of the Southwest. Department of Labor officials claim that the supply of new green-carders has been sharply curtailed since 1968. However, there are absolutely no statistics available to document this claim. Assuming the position is valid, the policy of refusing to issue—or at least sharply reducing the number of—*new* cards is a step in the right direction. Such a policy does not adversely affect those people who already have green cards, so the practice should arouse little ire from the Mexican government. On the other hand, as earlier discussion has shown, the exemptions from the labor certification process are so numerous that even if certification denials are increasing, the impact on the total number of crossers may be marginal.

Hopefully, the illusion that green-carders are no different from other resident immigrants has been put to rest. If some sort of commuter system has to exist for political reasons, there is no reason why it must continue in its present form. Many people have proposed that a new class of commuters be established. If legitimate and short-term labor shortages occur, a new card (in reality a work permit) could be granted for a specified time period. Unlike the present green card, the proposed card would not entail any future immigration commitment. The bearer of the card would be entitled to cross the border if he met prescribed standards. Obtaining such a card would not make the recipient a resident immigrant, nor would it provide any other family members or relatives the

75

right to eventual citizenship. Actually, for all intents and purposes, such a nonequity card already exists. It is known as an "H-2 visa" and is issued by the U.S. Department of State to meet demands for temporary workers under special circumstances. Under such an arrangement, it would be possible to regulate the supply of labor crossing the border.

As a necessary corollary, it is mandatory that all existing immigration laws be rigidly enforced along the southern border. Serious consideration should be given toward the launching of a drive to return illegal entrants already in the country back to Mexico. The so-called Texas proviso should be repealed and a new law making it illegal for employers to knowingly hire illegal entrants should be adopted. Careful checks should be made of all large employers in the rural Southwest to assure that social security taxes are actually being transmitted to the government.

Concurrently, foreign economic aid in the form of technical assistance and development loans should be made available to Mexico for the extensive development of the agricultural and industrial potential of its northern states. It is conceivable that a successful development strategy that is consistent with Mexico's similar desires (as manifested by PRONAF) could make the region less dependent upon the United States and simultaneously serve to reduce the existing outward migration pressure of the border area. A parallel effort of economic development on the American side of the border should also be given a high priority—especially by the Economic Development Administration. South of the border, there is a remorseful saying that "Mexico is so far from God yet so near to the United States." The pejorative implications of this adage to both nations could be partially mitigated if a comprehensive effort were made to develop simultaneously the economies on both sides of the border.

The isolation of workers employed in agriculture and small

business in the rural sectors from coverage of generally accepted social legislation in other sectors must end. They too deserve the minimum protection afforded by unemployment compensation, workmen's compensation, welfare safeguards, and comparable minimum wage and overtime pay guarantees with those set elsewhere in the economy. The original philosophical argument for the existence of these programs in non-agricultural industries has always been the simple proposition espoused by Edwin Witte, famed professor of economics at the University of Wisconsin in the 1930s: "It's good social policy." What is it that is different about an agricultural worker who is maimed while at work; or who is unemployed for fifteen weeks a year; or who is paid a lower wage for doing more arduous tasks for longer hours; or who is subject to arbitrary and unilateral treatment by an employer? The only distinction is that the law makes it so.

The usual excuse for making farmworkers the exception to every statutory enactment is often said to be that inclusion will hasten mechanization or that it will have inflationary effects upon the economy. As for the former, the rapid pace of mechanization is coming anyway. Indications are that the only barrier to the introduction of equipment is the time needed to perfect it. It has certainly not been a rise in labor costs that has provoked the accelerated substitution of capital for labor that has given agriculture the highest productivity increases of any industrial sector of the economy since 1947. As for inflation, it is simply impossible to lay the blame for higher food prices upon farmworkers. The cost of farm labor ranges from about 2 cents to 5 cents per dollar value of farm produce.[1] Thus, again, standard economic theory of factor pricing proves inadequate. For it is usually assumed that an item that is a small portion of total cost ought to be able to increase its factor income with little resistance—the so-called "importance of being unimportant" phenomenon. For farm labor, the theoretical proposition must be restated to read "the unimportance of being important."

Henry George wrote in the nineteenth century that the cost of production should include "the blood of the worker" (as his justification for the enactment of state Workmen's Compensation laws). Certainly, today the sweat of the worker should be compensated for at a level which will provide income above the poverty level. The annual 5 to 10 percent increases in farm productivity ought to be able to absorb easily the wage rates required to provide a humane standard of living *without any increase in consumer prices*. If they cannot, the conventional economic postulates that relate factor payments to factor productivity are in worse shape than even their most harsh critics have argued.

Because there are so few spokesmen for the rural poor, it is particularly important to encourage collective bargaining and the establishment of other representative organizations among rural workers. Many Chicano agricultural workers are employed by the nation's largest corporations—the agribusinesses which rule the industry of the Southwest. Workers should be given the protection to organize into unions if they so desire. It should be expected that wages would increase. In fact, to be successful in raising incomes, it is necessary (because of the seasonality of employment) to guarantee a minimum number of hours per day and a minimum number of weeks of work. The seasonality issue has long been recognized as a legitimate reason for high wages in construction work; it should become the similar pattern in agriculture. Agricultural labor costs will rise, but, if productivity continues to increase, unit labor costs should be affected little if at all. If costs are actually pushed upward, the fact that farm labor costs remain almost an inconsequential portion of total costs should mean that the effects upon final consumer prices would be hardly noticeable in a secularly inflationary economy.

In early 1971, proposals were made by southwestern regional manpower officials to the U.S. Department of Labor that were designed to alter the current neglect of rural manpower in general and Chicano rural manpower in particular. One recommendation was that state manpower funds be distributed in direct relation to the proportion that rural disadvantaged groups bear to the *total* disadvantaged population of the state. Migrant workers, in turn, would be given priority consideration in the disbursement of these funds made available to the rural needy. The second suggestion was that funds not apportioned to the states be set aside at the national level of the MDTA. The suggested amount of $50 million annually would be used to fund exceptional and exemplary migrant programs that do not receive funding under normal processes. Serious study should be given to these proposals for a set equity ratio.

The present distribution of manpower funds for rural areas is inadequate, and in many places of severe need manpower programs are nonexistent. Moreover, there is no doubt as to the need to develop innovative programs to deal with the unique problems of rural areas and the necessity of having local staff who are familiar with rural problems in general and local problems in particular. The surest way to see to it that rural areas get their fair share of manpower outlays is to earmark certain funds for this purpose. There are, however, some questions that need to be made clear before one accepts the proposal in its simplest form. One immediate problem is the assumption of an unreal dichotomy between rural and urban. Many people (especially Chicanos) live in urban areas and work in rural areas, and vice-versa. Similarly there are rural-urban interactions which make it difficult to determine where manpower money should be spent in specific cases. Another problem would be establishing a rationale for a rural quota of manpower money that was consistent with national manpower policies and objectives. A serious emphasis on manpower programs for rural areas will probably require larger expenditures than generated by the equity ratio. Clearly, there are insufficient funds at present to meet the needs in either rural or urban areas. It is likely that a better strategy would be to establish specific priorities which concentrate funds on particular objectives rather than a categorical allocation to rural or urban programs. A rural-urban split could introduce inflexibility rather than greater flexibility in the performance of the total manpower functions. Nevertheless, if the choice becomes one between a continuation of the prevailing allocation methods and procedures versus an equity ratio, the latter is clearly the better choice.

On the immediate horizon, the major policy uncertainty is the effect of the various welfare reform proposals that are being bandied about in Washington. The effect of these proposals on rural migration is far from clear. Better job information coupled with income maintenance may accelerate present out-migration trends. By removing the financial risks, the younger and better educated workers may move more readily. Conversely, the lower costs of living in rural areas may cause income maintenance recipients to return to rural areas as the rural-urban cost of living differentials are, in some instances, as large as 100 percent. The key to the answer may rest with the work test provision that is bound to be a feature of the ultimate program. Must people who are required to work in order to acquire benefits be relocated if there is no work within a commuting radius of their homes? As the answer is probably "no," a massive public employment program will be necessary to enforce the test in most southwestern rural areas.

Thus, in summary, all recent studies show that per capita family income is the principal determinant of education, health, housing, and leisure activities. Income for rural Chicanos flows almost exclusively from employment. A major factor in the denial of equal opportunities for Chicanos to secure income at above poverty levels is the unfair, unequal, and inequitable public policies that condition their employment experience. Currently there are jobs in both the agricultural and the rural nonfarm sectors which could provide income to thousands of people at above poverty levels if the institutional restrictions were removed. Such changes, in concert with a long overdue public effort to develop the human resource potential of the people, are what is needed. If they are both not forthcoming, full support should be given to income maintenance and public service employment proposals to bolster rural family incomes along with the full complement of supportive services necessary to overcome the prevailing Hobson's choice of moving to urban barrios.

Mañana es hoy.

NOTES

1. "Farm Workers," Staff Report Prepared for the U.S. Commission on Civil Rights, *Hearings* (Washington, D.C.: U.S. Government Printing Office, 1969), p. 964.

Library of Congress Cataloging in Publication Data

Briggs, Vernon M.
  Chicanos and rural poverty.

  (Policy studies in employment and welfare, no. 16) Includes biblio-
graphical references.
  1. Mexican Americans—Economic conditions—Southwestern States. 2.
Rural poor—Southwestern States. I. Title.
E184.M5B74   331.6'3'68   72-12370
ISBN 0–8018–1473–1
ISBN 0–8018–1472–1 (pbk)